D0893646

GERMAN WIREHAIRED POINTERS

TODAY

SHARON PINKERTON

New York

Maxwell Macmillan Canada
Toronto

Maxwell Macmillan International
New York Oxford Singapore Sydney

HOWELL BOOK HOUSE
A Prentice Macmillan Company
15 Columbus Circle
New York, NY 10023

MACMILLAN is a registered trademark of Macmillan, Inc.

Library of Congress Cataloging-in-Publication data

Pinkerton. Sharon.
  German wirehaired pointers today / by Sharon Pinkerton.

     p.   cm.
   ISBN 0-87605-182-4
   1. German wirehaired pointers.   I. Title
  SF429.G43P55   1994   94-9534   CIP
  636.7'52 – dc20

Manufactured in Singapore
10 9 8 7 6 5 4 3 2 1

CONTENTS

ACKNOWLEDGEMENTS

I would like to thank everyone who replied to my letters and forwarded material, all of which has been included. Additionally, a special thank-you to Peter Lomasney for his expertise on the working/falconry section, to Rudi Hulsman for his translating, to Arnold Steetskamp for the Dutch photographs/material, to Anne Johnson for her superb line drawings, and to Laura Myles who helped me to obtain the American material included.

A big thank-you to my parents, whose help enabled me to to find the time to write this book.

Lastly, an enormous thank-you to the German Wirehaired Pointer for being a very special breed of dog.

Chapter One

HISTORY OF THE BREED

EARLY ANCESTORS

The German Wirehaired Pointer, as the name suggests, originated in Germany where the breed is known as Drahthaar, the translation of Wirehair. It is a recent development in pure-bred dogs. An early ancestor is thought to be the Barbet, one of Europe's first rough-haired sporting dogs, supposedly developed from crosses between rough-haired sheepdogs, known as Schapudel, and smooth-coated hunting dogs, known as Bracke. In the beginning of the 19th century the Barbet, who had proved to be successful on all kind of game, both in water and over all types of ground, was crossed with other German sporting dogs and a new breed, known as the Ruehaar, was created. This name was later changed to Stichelhaar, which is more widely known today.

Prior to the late eighteenth century, German law restricted hunting, so it was a sport only enjoyed by a small, privileged group of people. However, towards the end of that century, and into the early nineteenth century, political changes within Germany opened the sport to a larger fraternity, so hunting became a more popular pastime. This meant that, as more and more people became involved, so they realised that there was a need to develop the existing German sporting dogs. These had already been split into groups described as shorthaired, longhaired and rough-haired. What was needed now was a breed that could trail, hunt and find game, point, and subsequently retrieve both wounded and dead game. It was necessary for the breed to be able work on command in variable terrain, have unlimited stamina and be capable of retrieving boldly from water. It was also required to work with game birds, rabbit, fox, deer and wild boar — truly an all-round sporting dog. It needed a combination of the speed, fine nose and staunch pointing of a Pointer, tracking and retrieving abilities, and a love of water, coupled with natural intelligence and a biddable nature.

THE ALL-ROUND SPORTING DOG

The lengthy process to develop this superior, all-round sporting dog began. Soon it was realised that the rough-haired dogs were ideal, due to their thick and wiry coat, which offered great protection from all kinds of weather and from the dense cover in which the dogs worked. The Griffon and Stichelhaar had the type of coat which was considered most desirable. However, the consensus was that these breeds had been produced more for exhibition than for performance and that many of the necessary abilities were sadly lacking.

At this stage crosses with Poodles and Pointers were introduced. The Poodles used were the German Pudel, a heavy-boned, sturdy sporting breed. This combination produced dogs with a high degree of intelligence, the natural ability of a Pointer and the sporting ability of the Pudel, thereby creating the well-known Pudel Pointer.

During 1873, in Germany, a Dutchman named Karel Eduard Korthals started breeding dogs that could be used for hunting. His methods of selection were hard. He had all pups that did not come up to his expectations put down. Nevertheless, he has been of great importance in the development of the Wirehair, and the creation of the breed is credited to him. Korthals founded the Griffon Club in 1883. His work in developing the Wirehair was followed by Freiherr Sigismund von Zedlitz und Neukirch, who was better known as Hegewald, the spiritual father of the Wirehair.

In 1892 the Deutsches Gebrauchshunde-Stammbuch – DGStB (German Versatile Hunting Dog Record Book) – was established, into which all the test results of all hunting dogs were entered annually. This book has become invaluable for all who are interested in hunting dogs. It is interesting to note that between 1892 and 1925 the number of German Wirehaired Pointers entered in the Record Book rose from two per cent to forty-seven per cent of all the entries. These figures are of those dogs who passed the Verbands Gebrauchs-Prufung – VGP (Versatile Hunting Dog Test).

On May 15th 1902, in Berlin, a group of sporting dog owners formed the Verein Deutsch Drahthaar (German Wirehaired Club). It was for everyone interested in all rough-coated sporting dogs and included experienced and skilled breeders. Lauffo Unkel am Rhein was elected President from the beginning and continued in office for thirty-two years. The Club stated: "The first thing to be obtained is perfection in hunting, next a good and suitable build, and finally beauty." Due to the freedom given when breeding – for example, the use of Stichelhaars, Griffons, Pudel Pointers and Shorthairs – it was not long before the first aim was achieved. It was, however, some years before they started to produce dogs with the correct physical structure. The problem was producing dogs with suitable thick and wiry coats. It was considered necessary to be very critical of the existing dogs and therefore it was very important to use only the best for breeding. In an attempt to control this factor, rules were made and the *Stammbuch Deutsch Drahthaar* (*German Wirehair Stud Book*) was introduced. The only dogs that could be registered in the Studbook were those over one year old to whom approval had been given regarding the correctness of coat, conformation and working ability in the field. The minimum age was later reduced to seven months. Dogs which had failed to gain approval in any aspect were refused registration and could not be used for breeding.

The hard fight for recognition continued. Eventually in 1928, after the Wirehairs had become the leading breed in sporting dogs, the German Kartell for Dogs accepted the membership of the German Wirehaired Club.

EXPANSION TO AMERICA

The breed arrived in the USA in the 1920s and, before long, was proving to be an excellent all-round gundog there also, but it was some thirty years later, in 1953, that the German Drahthaar Club of America was formed and accepted. Then, in 1959, the breed was granted

Typical German Wirehaired Pointers in the 1950s.

Championship status and admitted into the American Kennel Club Studbook, under the breed heading of the German Wirehaired Pointer. The first Wirehair to be accepted was called Eiko vom Schultenhof, who had been imported from Germany by W. D. Kyle, Jr. This liver and white ticked dog was sired by Bodo v.d. Hammer Mark out of Blanka vom Schoolenberg and was born in 1950. Once the AKC accepted the breed as the German Wirehaired Pointer instead of the German Drahthaar, a change of name for the club was necessary and the German Wirehaired Pointer Club of America was born.

THE FIRST ARRIVALS IN THE UK
It is known that a few Wirehairs were imported into Great Britain soon after the Second World War, having been brought back by members of the forces who had seen them in Germany. Unfortunately some of these were not registered with the Kennel Club. One of the first imports was a liver roan dog, called Klaus, who was brought into this Country by Captain L. B. Shelton on his return to Derbyshire after being stationed in Hamburg. This was a dog with a full wire coat who had been purchased, at three years of age, after being fully trained by a forester living near the Haseldorf Barracks, south of Hamburg.

Another was a bitch called Adda aus dem Potterhoek who was bred by Roland Buschung at Munster and imported by Godfrey Gallia in 1955. He bought her during his national service in Germany and trained her himself before she was imported at nine months old. Due to the lack of Wirehairs in Great Britain at this time and the fact that Klaus was found to be too old to successfully mate Adda aus dem Potterhoek, she, along with others, were bred with Shorthairs and therefore could not be regarded as true purebred German Wirehaired Pointers. It was unfortunate that a granddaughter of Adda, which Godfrey Gallia retained, was not registered with the Kennel Club owing to the rules regarding cross bred dogs, because her line included German Shorthaired Pointers originating from a dog called Ch. Blitz of Longsutton.

THE DUTCH CONNECTION

1959 saw the founding, in Holland, of the Vereniging Vrienden Duits Draadhaar. This Club was not an immediate success and, because of a lack of members, nearly closed down. The revival was due to an important figure in the Dutch gundog world called Arend Jacob Van Buuren, who was one of the leading judges of both field and show dogs and a great supporter of the Wirehair He played an active part in the VVDD after taking over as Secretary in 1963 and eventually became its Chairman.

Holland, like Germany, has a strict breeding strategy. The VVDD has a Breeding Advisory Committee which requires certain standards to be met before any programme is allowed to start. Generally this means that both Wirehairs must not be HD positive, they must have attained a minimum 'Very Good' qualification for their conformation and they must have qualified in field matches. Provided that both dog and bitch have gained the necessary requirements, the breeder can then obtain a breed certificate. The VVDD will only advertise 'qualified puppies' from these matings, consequently there is usually a shortage. The VVDD claim that the advantages of their breeding strategy are that the breeder is virtually certain of selling the puppies, the new owners know their background, and the chances of failure are supposed to be minimal.

BACK TO BRITAIN

The breed was re-introduced into Great Britain in l972 by a liver and white bitch called Vrede Von Romersee, who was selected by Herr Alfons Wischerhoff for a friend of Major George Wilkinson. Major Wilkinson himself trained gundogs and was the inspiration behind the establishment of Wirehairs in the UK. The friend, Bill Warner, soon realised that she was just what he had wanted, which was a superb working gundog. It was at this point that they realised that there was no turning back and they had to continue to produce excellent working gundogs, such as Vrede. With a view to breeding with her, they decided to contact the Kennel Club to enquire what other Wirehairs were registered. Unfortunately the Kennel Club could only come up with the fact that there was just one registered Wirehair in the country and that was a dog called Chang, owned by a gamekeeper called Mr Meredith, and he had been registered on the class II registration in 1970. On checking his breeding, they realised that he was a grandson of Adda aus dem Potterhoek and the brother of the bitch that Godfrey Gallia had decided not to register. Although Chang was a typical Wirehair in appearance and had proved to be an excellent worker, they decided that he was not really suitable because he had Shorthair blood in his immediate ancestry.

Major Wilkinson and Bill Warner decided to contact Herr Wischerhoff again with a view to importing new stock, especially a male in order to breed with Vrede. This time they went to the Bocholter kennel, who specialised in black and whites. They returned with a litter brother and sister, namely Vassel and Vicky v.d. Bocholter. These dogs were registered in 1974 and are the ancestors of all the black and white Wirehairs in Great Britain.

Tony Vaughan, who knew the breed in Belgium, had been impressed with the looks and working ability of Vicky and decided to approach Major Wilkinson in an effort to obtain two unrelated Wirehairs from Germany. Unfortunately Major Wilkinson was not able to

Bill Warner's original bitch, Vrede Von Romersee.

Mieneke Mills de Hoog's original import, Matilde Vant Staringsland to Wittekind.

Tony Vaughan's Dutch imported bitch, Heliose.

spare the time, but suggested that Tony should contact Mieneke Mills de Hoog and ask her to select the dogs from Holland. Mieneke, who is Dutch and who was already well established in German Shorthaired Pointers, accepted this request and, in addition to the two Wirehairs for Tony, imported a bitch for herself. The Dutch dogs were found to be a little longer in coat than most of the German dogs, but they had superb working abilities coupled with show qualities. The unrelated pair brought in for Tony were Rakker v.d. Mijzijde and

Heliose; the bitch that Mieneke brought in was Matilde Vant Staringsland to Wittekind.

This unrelated trio, registered in 1975, actually formed the basis of the famous Wittekind line. At about this time, Mr and Mrs Burnham returned to England from serving in Germany and brought back with them their bitch Hedda Von Der Reiherbeize. She was registered in 1975 and, later in that year, she was bred to Mr Meredith's Chang and produced the Matraver line.

By this time the interest in the German Wirehaired Pointer was steadily growing, so on the February 29th 1976 a meeting of German Wirehaired Pointer enthusiasts was called by Major Wilkinson at his kennels on the Land of Nod Estate, Headley Down, Surrey. Nine Wirehairs turned up. They were Vicky v.d. Bocholter, Vassel v.d. Bocholter, Rakker v.d. Mijzijde, Heliose, Matilde Vant Staringsland to Wittekind and four half-grown pups from the Vassel and Vrede litter, bred by Bill Warner. These were in addition to Major Wilkinson's own dogs and his three-week-old litter from Vicky v.d. Bocholter to Rakker v.d. Mijzijde. This informal gathering of dogs and owners was a great success. It continued in a more formal fashion at Hindhead, with the fourteen people present agreeing to form a Club and to apply to the Kennel Club for recognition.

GROWTH OF INTEREST
By the late 1970s the number of pure-bred Wirehairs being registered was growing and more and more people were showing an interest in the breed. In 1976 Wittekind Amigo was exported to Mr W. Krahnen in Australia and, during 1977, a bitch called Wittekind Britt followed. Also during 1977 a dog and bitch were exported to Mr J. Dawson in New Zealand. These were Wittekind Auslage, litter brother to Wittekind Amigo, who went on to become a New Zealand Champion, and Alice of Kenstaff. They were closely followed by Basco v.d. Andesheim who also went out to join Mr J. Dawson and later became a New Zealand Champion.

Unfortunately it was at this time that the two German imports to the UK, Vassel v.d. Bocholter and Vicky v.d. Bocholter, had to be put down. Although they appeared to have come through quarantine without problems, they actually had great trouble adjusting to their new life-style and became very anti-social towards other dogs. At this stage both had bred one litter, and the progeny, fortunately, seemed to be of excellent temperament.

IMPROVING THE BREED
As most of the early stock in the UK were direct descendants of the Dutch imports, the majority suffered with far from perfect coats (woolly coats) and a temperament bordering on sharpness, even though the working capability was still excellent. In an attempt to improve the breed construction further, without losing any of the good points, it became obvious that more new blood was needed.

In order to broaden the breed's base, Major Wilkinson decided to import another bitch, preferably in whelp, to enable a wider spread of the bloodlines in the UK. On this occasion he enlisted the help of Herr Dr Tabel, who was the ex-President of the parent Club of Germany. Herr Tabel selected a bitch from Dr Robert Hoffman's Reiler Hals Kennels and Sissi vom Reiler Hals Andesheim arrived in October 1979, heavily in whelp. She had been mated to Baron vom Reiler Hals who had been first, out of sixty-one dogs, in a Field Trial in Germany and sixteenth, out of fifty-one dogs, in the Wirehair International in Austria, prior to being mated with Sissi. Dr Hoffman was the Breedmeister of the Mittelrhein branch of the Verein Deutsch Drahthaar, and the Reiler Hals kennels were especially noted for good temperament and excellent working ability. Unfortunately the whelping was traumatic and disappointing. Out of thirteen puppies born, only four survived, three bitches and one dog. A bitch and the dog puppy went to Mr and Mrs Durman Walters, one bitch went to John Birth and the other bitch went to Mr A. Barron in Northern Ireland. The next import arrived in February 1980, a liver and white male called Mr Allround of Wittekind, brought in by Mieneke Mills de Hoog from Sweden. Her prime reason for importing him was to add substance and bone to the existing British stock and improve the temperament and the coats. In addition he was HD free and came from HD free lines. Tragically he died in January 1982, but it was fortunate that he had already passed on to his progeny the desired improvements.

Lanka Bella Vom Insul, bred by Bill Warner, sired by Vassel v.d. Bocholter and out of Vrede Von Romersee.

Finally, after five years of perseverance, the Kennel Club agreed, in May 1981, to recognise the Club, and so the German Wirehaired Pointer Club was officially formed. In September 1982 Mr and Mrs Peter Howard imported a dog from the United States of America called Desert Mills Henry Tickencote (liver and white), aged only fifteen weeks. Although valuable time was lost due to quarantine, once released he was able to commence his training. This has been done successfully, with awards in both show and Field Trials and he has passed his abilities on to his progeny. In 1983 another dog went out to Mr P. Dawson in New Zealand and this was Dawsons English Connection.

In April 1984 the Bareve kennel (which I own in partnership with my mother, Barbara Pinkerton), imported another dog from the United States of America, called American Champion Geronimos Knickers Von S G at Bareve (liver and white). He

Mieneke Mills de Hoog's Swedish import Mr Allround of Wittekind.

was purchased as a four month old puppy but left in America for his breeder to show him to his title and to commence his training in the field. Although he was not worked by his owners, on his release from quarantine after travelling to the UK he has proved his working ability by passing it on to his progeny. Both these American dogs, although entirely unrelated, are descendants of a combined pedigree with numerous Show Champions and well tested working dogs.

In late 1983 Mieneke Mills de Hoog imported another dog, this time from Holland, and his name was Macdevil Van De Bemmeraue-Wittekind (liver and white). He was just over three months old, the progeny of a father and daughter mating. The father was Dutch Field Trial Champion Quell Von Der Wupperaue, a German-bred dog who had achieved the Hegewald Auslage Prufung Bestanden at only nineteen months of age, the most important test of work in Germany for Wirehairs. Unfortunately he contracted parvovirus and became desperately ill in quarantine and, although he made a full recovery, due to his tender age his bone and general substance were affected. But he too was able to pass on his working ability to his progeny.

In 1985 Mr and and Mrs L. Durman Walters and Mrs H. Hilson selected and imported two unrelated dogs from Germany. They were Arko V Billetal (solid liver) and Falk v Valkenhus (liver and white). Their pedigrees contain stock with proven working ability and they have shown that their attributes are passed on to their progeny. In 1987 Wiggmansburg Amigo was exported to Mr M. Somers in New Zealand and he too became a New Zealand Champion.

In 1989 Lady Graham Moon imported an unrelated male and female from Germany called Asko v.d. Wurdemannshof and Herra vd Kalkuhle. They produced three puppies soon after coming out of quarantine whilst the bitch was under eighteen months of age. Having lived and worked with Labrador Retrievers, Lady Moon soon found the Wirehairs rather too much of a handful and so sent them to Mr P. Howard for training. Unfortunately the male was tragically killed whilst working, although the bitch has gone on to breed again.

Also imported from Germany was a bitch called Betty von Haverland owned by Major P. Cox who bought her whilst stationed in Germany. She was bought from a local hunter as a young adult having already commenced her working. Major Cox worked her in Germany before she was sent over to England and since quarantine she has continued to work during the shooting season.

Chapter Two

INSPECTION AND SELECTION

CHARACTERISTICS

As you have seen from reading the history and origins of the Wirehair, the breed is primarily for hunting and consequently requires great drive, tenacity and stamina to find quarry in all types of terrain. The typical Wirehair is medium-sized and rough-coated, capable of answering the all-round demands of sportsmen whether for common field rabbit and bird shooting, or the woodland shooting of birds and furred animals or even of waterfowl over marshes and open water. Wirehairs can also be trained for deer stalking and falconry.

The Kennel Club recognises that the Gundog Group has to be split into several parts because of the specific working abilities of the different breeds. For example there are

Am. Ch. Weidenhugel Capuccine: The German Wirehaired Pointer was bred to do a job of work and excels as an all-round gundog.

MikRon Photos.

Spaniels, Retrievers, Setters, Pointers and then the Hunting, Pointing and Retrieving breeds (HPR). The Wirehair is part of this group. Briefly this means that the Wirehair must be capable of hunting fearlessly through all forms of cover from low stubble to dense gorse bushes and brambles. By the use of excellent scenting ability the Wirehair should be able to indicate where the quarry is and hold that position. It is this indication which gives us the term 'on point'. The next stage is for the Wirehair, on command, to flush the game, to remain steady and then to adopt either a sitting or a down position, which enables the quarry to be shot without harm to others. Hopefully the shot will find its target and the handler can then send the Wirehair to retrieve it.

The German Wirehaired Pointer is still one of the few gundog breeds which has not developed a definite split between those dogs that can work and those capable of winning in the show ring. We can and do produce typical-looking Wirehairs with the ability to work, rather than Wirehairs with that ability but sadly lacking in breed type and so giving the impression of perhaps being of unknown breeding. This is important. Consequently conscientious breeders are striving to produce Wirehairs with 'beauty and brains' to maintain the breed as one type.

TEMPERAMENT

As the basic characteristics of the German Wirehaired Pointer are inherent, it is almost certain that these will come to the fore in the typical Wirehair. It is essential that these natural urges are controlled and channelled into the way of life that you choose, otherwise there is little doubt that you will experience problems. German Wirehaired Pointers are naturally very intelligent and show a great keenness to try and co-operate with their owners. The breed makes excellent companions for people who want to spend time with their dogs because of the alert and affectionate nature of Wirehairs, but they do not make particularly good kennel dogs because of a strong desire to be included in all activities. Wirehairs are extremely devoted to and extremely protective of the owner and the family.

It is common for German Wirehaired Pointers to be aloof with strangers, definitely preferring to be in the company of those known to them. This protectiveness has obvious advantages and disadvantages depending on the individual owner's circumstances and point of view but there is no doubt that the German Wirehaired Pointer is not to be recommended solely as a guard dog.

The Wirehair does respond well to training providing it is fair and coupled with a sense of discipline. A Wirehair requires a purpose in life and is easily bored if lacking the attention needed to stimulate the mind. Wirehairs are sensitive and do not take well to harsh correction. The breed is also prone to stubbornness, but this is generally because the necessary basic discipline has been neglected or there is confusion over what the owner or handler requires. Occasionally you will have a young German Wirehaired Pointer test your instructions by being stubborn. It is usually males who do this. The reason is that you have failed to be firm enough with your Wirehair at an earlier age and now your dog is challenging your position of being the "top dog". It is at this point that you will have to be much firmer and insist that when you ask your Wirehair to do something, it is done. On the whole, German Wirehaired Pointers are late maturing and need a very active lifestyle so that

Jack and Laura Myles' Am. Ch. Inverness Just In Time winning the Best of Winners at the 1984 SeaTac Specialty: The good-looking Wirehair has found favour in the show ring, but this must not be at the expense of the breed's working ability.

Carl Lindemaier.

the breed's sense of humour can be enjoyed to the full and there is not a constant battle of wits.

PHYSICAL APPEARANCE

The main characteristic of the Wirehair, which sets the breed apart from so many others, is the distinctive wiry coat. The outer coat is thick, harsh, completely covering the body, close fitting, and of a reasonable length, usually not longer than one and a half inches. Underneath the top layer is a dense softer undercoat which helps to protect and insulate, consequently this is more abundant in the winter than in the summer months. The eyebrows are bushy, and the muzzle must have a full but not over-long beard to complete the distinctive picture of the German Wirehaired Pointer.

Another essential characteristic of the breed is for the body length to exceed slightly the overall height. You will therefore have a dog a little longer in the body compared to the

Silke Albert's Am. Ch. Weidenhugel Cappucine and two of her progeny. Breeders are striving to avoid a split between working Wirehairs and show Wirehairs by producing dogs with brains as well as beauty.   *Callea Photography.*

Shargleam Rudesheim in the foreground, Bareve Bemyca, Kyle the Golden Retriever, and Bareve Bacall. The well-reared Wirehair has a superb temperament and will fit in well with all members of the family – both human and canine.

John Hartley.

height at the shoulders, a ten to nine ratio. As you will see from the diagram, the length of body relates to ten and the height at the shoulder relates to nine. The breed must not be short in body as this would resemble a German Shorthaired Pointer's square outline which is a ten to ten ratio as the diagram shows. The German Wirehaired Pointer is a totally separate and distinct breed from the German Shorthaired Pointer. A Wirehair is most certainly not a wire-coated Shorthaired Pointer, as some people seem to think.

MAKING THE CHOICE

You must always consider carefully all the implications of owning a dog. Learn as much about German Wirehaired Pointers as you can before making any decisions. Remember this is very important because, with reasonable luck, you will have this member of your household for many years to come.

You have got to ask yourself the following questions:-

1. What do you want to do with your German Wirehaired Pointer?
2. Do you really need or want a German Wirehaired Pointer?

3. Do you know what they are like in real life or have you only seen them in books?

4. Have you got sufficient time to devote to training your puppy to ensure that your puppy will become a pleasure to live with?

5. Have you sufficient space to keep your German Wirehaired Pointer happy, or are you prepared to find the space needed?

6. Have you got unlimited patience to cope with the chaos and possible damage a puppy might do while learning to be clean and well-behaved?

If you have any doubts answering the questions positively then it is my suggestion that you reconsider the idea of being the owner of a Wirehair. You do need to be totally committed to the welfare and upbringing of this special breed.

If, however, you have answered all the questions and are still really keen to own one then you have various options available to you. Please do not rush out and buy the first cute, appealing puppy you see. Give yourself time to look at as many of the breed as you can before you decide. At this stage you must consider what in fact you wish to do. Do you want to work your Wirehair and compete in Field Trials? Do you want to show your Wirehair and, if so, at what level do you wish to compete? Do you want to do obedience or working trials? Do you want a foundation bitch to develop your own line or do you want just a family dog as a companion? Whatever your intentions, it is essential that your Wirehair is well reared, healthy and comes from the best well-bred stock with which you are happy.

PRELIMINARY STEPS

One of the first things I suggest a prospective buyer does is to join a German Wirehaired Pointer breed club (in fact, there is only one in the UK). These clubs are formed for all owners of the breed, and not just for the dog-showing or the working fraternities. The clubs produce newsletters which will enable you to read all about forthcoming events and will also keep you in touch with any happenings in the breed. So, contact the national Kennel Club, which keeps an up-to-date list of all breed club secretaries, and then you can apply for a membership form.

At this point you could ask the secretary if there are any puppies being advertised on the club's puppy list, and if you can obtain details of those. Additionally you could ask if there are publications listing the breeders in the country. At the time of writing, there only a few of what people would really describe as breeders in the UK. There are, however, many more people who actually own bitches of this wonderful breed, and at some time they may consider having a litter. The main reason for this seems to be that it enables the owners to retain a puppy who will grow up with the mother and eventually take her place when she starts to age. Do not expect to be able to purchase a puppy immediately, after all, the Wirehair is still quite an unusual breed and consequently there are not always puppies available. It is not unusual to be put on to a waiting list, as most reputable owners will not consider having a litter until there are at least four to six definite homes waiting for a puppy.

As the breed is still quite new in this country it is usual to have different 'types' of German Wirehaired Pointers, although they are still considered pure-bred. Different lines produce different types. For example some lines produce bigger dogs, some produce smaller and lighter dogs, some produce dogs that are longer in coat with profuse furnishings, and others are shorter in coat with few furnishings. So the best advice I can give is to go and see as many German Wirehaired Pointers as you can, before you decide where you are going to purchase your puppy.

MEETING THE WIREHAIR

Probably the biggest collection of German Wirehaired Pointers to be found together will be at a Club Championship Show or Specialty. There are many other general Championship shows throughout the year, where the breed will be exhibited.

Be prepared to spend the whole day at the show. After all you are talking about a dog that is going to share your life for many years. If you make a bad choice because you could not afford to spare the time to watch and meet the breed, then you will always have only yourself to blame. Arrive at the show before judging starts and buy a catalogue. This will give you details of all the Wirehairs entered, with information on breeding and, most important, the names and addresses of the exhibitors. Position yourself at the ringside so that you can see all the exhibits as they enter the ring, as well as those that are waiting to go into each particular class. Then it is all down to watching and taking notes of those Wirehairs which catch your eye. If any of the Wirehairs seem especially attractive and you want to go across and get a closer look, then do so. Just a word of warning: you must remember that sometimes the exhibitors are busy getting ready, so please do ask if they have the time to spare to answer your questions or if they could suggest when it would be convenient. There are very few exhibitors who would turn down a request from someone who is interested in learning about the breed.

If you wish to purchase a puppy for working and Field Trials, and you do not want to spend time at a dog show, then there are still opportunities for you to see the breed. The obvious choice is one of the Gundog parades that are held in conjunction with most Game Fairs and Country Fairs. At these events there is usually a special tent set aside and properly benched, specifically so that the general public can view the breeds participating in the parades at close hand. Again, this will give you the opportunity to meet the Wirehairs and to ask the owners all the questions that you want answered about the breed. Also you might see other German Wirehaired Pointers being walked around at these events with their owners and if any of these impress you then ask where the Wirehair came from.

The other working events where you will, with luck, see German Wirehaired Pointers are Field Trials and Working Tests. These events are not usually publicly advertised. As the majority of members are not interested in competing in this sphere, management committees usually decide to save on money and administration by compiling special lists restricted to those they know are possible competitors.

Field Trials are an excellent way of seeing all breeds of dogs working under similar conditions to those at a shoot. Unfortunately there are, for spectators, some disappointing elements with these events. Most of the followers are kept behind various flag-carrying helpers so as not to interfere with the exhibits that are working and competing in the Field Trial. This means that at some trials you could actually be quite a distance away from the action. There is also always a limit on the number of dogs that can actually compete. Most

Field Trials are over-subscribed and this nearly always means that a draw has to be made to determine the actual competitors. This might mean that out of a maximum of twelve dogs competing, there might only be one German Wirehaired Pointer, if that. Another problem is that it is a competition based on the individual exhibit's working abilities on that day under those conditions. Dogs are not machines and even the best dog might have an off day, make a silly error and be technically "put out". So where Field Trials are concerned you might not actually get to see a tremendous amount.

Working Tests are events where various 'exercises' are set up in advance in an attempt to test the competing dogs' abilities and to mark them accordingly. More dogs are able to compete because of the exercises being pre-set rather than having all the dogs working on untouched ground as in Field Trials. The events are much more accessible to spectators and, as Working Tests are not considered as serious a competition as a Field Trial, it usually means that if an error is made the competitor is usually allowed to continue, as part of a learning process, rather than being "put out" as in Field Trials. This means that you would probably see more dogs in action at Working Tests than at Field Trials.

Having spent a day or at least some time with the breed, you will arrive home with a list of those Wirehairs that have caught your eye. Now is the time to study the breeding and breeders to see if any of them actually come from the same line. If you do end up establishing that those which appealed to you do come from the same line, then you will have achieved something.

VISITING THE BREEDER

Having decided on the line you like, your next step is to contact the breeder or the person producing it. Find out when it would be convenient to visit their Wirehairs at home, rather than at a show or a working event. It is best to telephone first to make an appointment as many people have set routines for their dogs and like to have visitors arrive at quiet times and not during feeding or exercise. Do not turn up unannounced. During this initial contact the caring breeder will question you in detail as to why you want a Wirehair. You may feel that this is a little impertinent but it is one of the ways in which breeders can determine whether you are genuine or are wasting their time. Remember that it is the breeder's responsibility to find the correct homes for the Wirehairs they produce and they will do their absolute best to ensure that this happens.

If there is a litter due then you will have the opportunity to meet the prospective mother. If you are visiting one of the more established breeders then there is every chance of seeing a number of the breed. Do not be surprised if you are unable to see the stud dog. Caring breeders are always trying to improve the breed so consequently they would not necessarily use a stud dog who lives down the road, just for convenience. Breeders will use what they consider to be the best stud dog for their own line, which might mean that the stud dog does not belong to the breeder or even live locally. Breeders who have nothing to hide will be only too pleased to show you all of their stock, including those considered to be pet quality or those who are getting older and are probably no longer being exhibited. Anybody who hides dogs away is doing it for a reason, possibly because of poor quality or suspect temperament so that the dog cannot be trusted to meet strangers.

Do not confuse bad temperament with barking, as there are few places strangers can enter without the Wirehairs in residence barking a warning. If you are in doubt then look at the Wirehair involved. Is the barking accompanied by a wagging tail, or are the eyes narrowed, the coat on the back standing up and the tail down? The first display is normal at the arrival of a stranger. If however you are met by a Wirehair showing the second set of mannerisms then in my eyes you are being warned off. Once you have been introduced to the Wirehairs, there should be no signs of aggression and any such display must be treated with suspicion.

Having said that, you must remember that the breed can be aloof with strangers and this must not be confused with aggression. Aloofness is when a dog will seem to be reserved and will probably not like a very direct approach by a stranger. If this is the case and you then choose to ignore the Wirehair, in no time at all you will be approached and a friendship formed – but it will have been done the Wirehair's way.

Look at the condition of the Wirehairs around you. Do they look healthy and in good condition? Do they look happy? Then ask yourself if you are still happy with that particular type. Do you like the temperament of the Wirehairs and especially that of the prospective mother of the puppies? Do not forget to ask questions about the breed in general and anything else that you want to know.

CHOOSING A PUPPY

Now you will have to decide if you want a puppy from this strain and, if so, how long you will have to wait for one. If a breeder actually has a bitch in whelp there might, as I have said before, be a waiting list for prospective buyers. If this is the case, you may ask if you can be put on the list to be contacted when the litter has safely arrived. Do not automatically expect to have either the first or second pick of a litter. There might be people who have been waiting for a puppy for a much longer time, and the litter may well have been planned to enable the breeder to retain one or more of the puppies. If that is the case nobody who has gone through all the trouble and expense of rearing a litter will then let someone come in and choose a puppy that the breeder wants to keep.

If you are not prepared to wait for a puppy from the kennel of your choice, then it will be up to you to decide the next step. You can of course refer back to the other Wirehairs you have seen and contact one of the owners whose stock you also liked. Additionally, litters of puppies are regularly advertised in dog papers and in shooting and countryside magazines. If you actually contact a person via an advertisement it is always a good idea to obtain as much information as possible about the litter and its parents before setting off to visit them. If a well-known stud dog has been used, contact the owner and ask whether the bitch has a good temperament and is a typical specimen of the breed. If you feel quite happy with the answers then a visit to see the litter would be a good idea. One word of warning: if you intend to compete with your puppy, either in the show ring or in the field, please insist on and check that the bitch is registered with your national Kennel Club and the litter is either KC registered or able to be before purchasing a puppy. It would not be the first time that someone has bought a puppy to show from an advert, only to find that the puppy had not been registered because the mother was unable to be registered.

Most respected breeders will not allow anybody to see their puppies until they are five to

A typical thirteen-week-old puppy – note the few whiskers around the muzzle.

six weeks old. This is because of the possible risk of bringing in infection into the puppy quarters, and because nobody will risk upsetting the mother, who could desert the puppies if there is interference by strangers. Also, to prevent any possible spread of infection, it is good manners and good sense not to visit different kennels on the same day without taking the precaution of a complete change of clothing and footwear.

At between five and six weeks puppies are just starting to become individuals, as each character begins to develop. The puppies will also have been weaned and will be more used to being handled. At this age the puppies become more active with growth, the coats start to develop and the colour begins to darken. German Wirehaired Pointers are actually born clear liver and white or clear black and white. The ticking and roaning comes at a much later date. Be prepared to see some variance within the litter. Do not forget that the breed is still relatively new outside its native country and, with the mixture of bloodlines available, it is no surprise to see different types of puppies within the one litter. Some may have quite a full coat, some may look almost bald, some may be light in colour and some dark.

The actual choice of puppy will have to depend on what your intentions are. Nobody can guarantee a show-quality puppy at such an early age. Show potential is a different thing. There are so many things that could possibly go wrong with a growing puppy that I defy anybody to guarantee that a seven week old puppy has show quality. Nobody can predict the future and it would not be the first time that a show-quality puppy has been badly reared to such a degree that the early promise has failed to be fulfilled. No one can be certain of being able to pick the best puppy at this early stage. After all, in one of our litters, where people had eight dog puppies to choose from, the one that was constantly overlooked and eventually left behind, went on to be one of our Show Champions.

If you are looking for a puppy with show potential then my advice is to listen to the breeder, unless you are experienced in dogs in general. And when you are viewing, ask the breeder to separate those puppies which have already been booked from those still available so that you know that if you find the puppy you really want, that puppy can be yours.

INSPECTING A PUPPY

One of the first things to check is the puppy's mouth. Even at this stage the teeth should meet cleanly, with the top row of teeth slightly overlapping the bottom row. The bite must not be either undershot or overshot. Both are considered faults, and the puppy should only be sold as a pet, and should not be bred from, if either imperfection is present. Of the two, the overshot mouth is considered the less serious because, as the puppy grows, the bottom jaw alters. In some cases where a puppy has had a slight overshot bite at ten weeks old, after a year the bite will have become a scissor bite. Unfortunately, because of the way the bottom jaw alters, an undershot mouth will always become much worse as the puppy grows.

Check the puppy's eyes. Obviously make sure that they have not got an infection, but it is even more more important to check the eyelids. Do they fit correctly? Do the lids roll inwards or outwards? If they do either, then, unfortunately, it would seem that the puppy has either entropion or ectropion. If you have gone to an experienced breeder then the chances of being offered a puppy with eye problems will be minimal, as most breeders who are unfortunate enough to have this problem will know that the puppy will have to be retained at this stage.

Both conditions are very serious hereditary eye defects which will cause the puppy a lot of discomfort. Consequently the puppy should eventually only be sold as a pet, with the Kennel Club registration endorsed as having been either spayed or castrated, to ensure the condition is not passed on. It is not life-threatening and most vets will be able to operate and repair the eyelids when the puppy is about six months old. After the operation and recuperation, the Wirehair will soon realise that all the discomfort has disappeared and that a perfectly normal lifestyle lies ahead. Most puppies at this early age will have quite a light blue-grey eye colour. This is quite normal as the colour of the eyes will continue to darken right up to full maturity. Unfortunately this does not mean that there are no light eyes in the breed, but even those will darken considerably through age. If you are choosing a male puppy, then do remember to check and make sure that both testicles can be felt. Even though at such a young age they might not have dropped, you should still be able to feel them.

Hopefully, after checking these main points, there will still be a choice of puppies available. Now is the time when you have to assess overall conformation combined with correct coat. It is no good having a well-constructed puppy with an incorrect coat or vice versa. It is helpful at this stage if the puppies are made to stand on a table to assess their conformation. Providing of course the puppies co-operate, you will be able to see their overall shape. Remember that one of the breed requirements is for the length of body to be a little longer than the overall height, as ten is to nine. Therefore do not choose a puppy with a short body and long legs, as the resulting adult will be of incorrect breed type. You should be looking for an adult's shape reduced to a puppy's size.

Coats are more difficult to assess. The ideal to look for at this stage would be short and close-fitting, with just a few whiskers on the muzzle. This coat type when fully mature should be hard and wiry, with undercoat, but will not become too long and untidy. You do not want to see a totally smooth coat with no whiskers, as this type will probably end up being like a German Shorthaired Pointer, totally devoid of coat. This is a very serious fault. Although you are looking for a short coat, you should still be able to feel, even on a seven week old puppy, that it is wiry to the touch. Possibly the litter from which you are making your choice might not have any puppies with the ideal coat. Even so, a puppy whose coat is flat but a little long in length, with a whiskery face, is still a good choice. Any puppies that already have quite long coats and a mass of whiskers, will be quite heavy-coated when mature. Although this coat type is probably more appealing, unless you are prepared to spend a lot of time stripping the long coat out, you will always have an 'open coat'. This is the expression for a coat which will not lie flat because of its length and so will not be as water-tight and weather-resistant as a correct wiry, tight-fitting coat. Obviously, if you are not looking for a puppy with show potential then a heavier-coated puppy would not cause any problems, and as I have already said, would probably be more appealing.

The other extreme of texture is what we call a 'woolly coat'. This was a great problem in the early days, when so many German Wirehaired Pointers were of Dutch-bred stock. As time has gone on, and we have bred further away from those originals using new imports with better coats, there has been a dramatic improvement. In those early days it was quite common to have complete litters of woolly coats, but now, fortunately, this is not so frequent. We still do have woolly-coat puppies born but they are very apparent from an early age. Even in the nest it is possible to assess if there is a woolly coat, as it seems to alter daily, getting longer and turning wavy. By the time puppies are of an age to be sold they are very obvious. The puppy will have a very long coat (about an inch long would not be uncommon) and it would be wavy, with a silky, soft feel to it. The puppy's face would be very hairy and even the ears would have a fringe around them. There again, if you wanted a pet puppy, a woolly-coated puppy should not put you off. All it means is that from an early age you would have to get the puppy used to being either clippered or scissored, so that the coat could be kept to a manageable length.

The other point to remember is temperament. All puppies of this age should be bold and approach you fearlessly, with upright or wagging tails giving the appearance of mischievous youngsters. There will always be some that are already showing signs of being the "top dog", and those puppies will always be at the front of the action. However, at seven weeks, the character of puppies will not really have developed because of still being in the nest in the whelping quarters. Once a puppy leaves the nest it is up to you to develop the character as the puppy grows. Whatever your Wirehair is at six months old will be entirely your doing, rightly or wrongly.

If you are choosing a puppy for working, all the points I consider important for a show-potential puppy are just as important for a working dog. The Wirehair is a dual-purpose gundog, who combines beauty with brains, and we must continue to do our utmost to maintain that. You might just as well have a good-looking Wirehair working and competing as one who fails to come up to a typical standard. I dislike hearing that people want working-bred puppies for working and do not want a puppy that has been produced from show stock. As I have said previously, a seven week old puppy has no developed character but does have an abundance of ability and intelligence. If people cannot train a German Wirehaired Pointer to do what they want, then I am afraid it is because of the person in question and not the Wirehair. There have been many cases of adult German Wirehaired Pointers being retired, for various reasons, from the show ring and then, at this late stage, commencing training on the working side and going on to win places in Field Trials. This proves that the breed has got the natural ability to work and, as in so many things, it is all down to the owner to achieve it.

Once you have decided on your choice, provided the puppy is at least seven weeks old, is fully weaned and has been wormed, it is time to go to the new home. Most caring breeders will let you have at least a week's supply of the puppy food they have been using, together with a detailed diet sheet. It is essential that you continue to use the food that the puppy has been used to, because changing homes causes enough trauma without having a changed diet at the same time.

It is a good idea to have someone with you when you collect your puppy to ensure that the puppy travels as safely and as comfortably as possible. It is better for the puppy to travel either on someone's lap or beside them on the seat. The puppy will feel happier being held and so restrained from leaping off the seat onto the car floor. An old towel is always useful to take along in case the puppy should be travel-sick. Most puppies will have never been in a car before, so make sure that the first car-ride is as comfortable as possible so that it becomes something to accept and enjoy, rather than something to fear.

Chapter Three

UPBRINGING

Before you actually bring the puppy home, it would be sensible to spend time ensuring that your house and garden are safe, secure and totally dog-proof. Not only will this stop your precious puppy escaping, it will also ensure that no stray and unwanted dogs can enter your garden and bring in infections before your puppy's vaccinations are complete. All dangerous objects and valuables in the house must be removed. Your puppy will not be able to distinguish between leather shoes – the pride of the owner – and a plaything put out specially for the new arrival.

It is also a good idea to fence off stairs with a guard gate such as the ones which prevent young children from using the stairs. Stairs are just as dangerous to any puppy. The least that could happen is for your Wirehair puppy to climb safely up and then find that the journey down is so frightening that the only option is to sit and cry until someone comes to the rescue. Far worse, if your Wirehair puppy is very bold and actually falls down the stairs, it can cause irreparable damage and very large vet bills.

KENNELLING
Ideally your Wirehair puppy will live with your family in the house. The breed rarely thrives living outside in a kennel, which involves leading a very separate life without the guidance of a human. Occasionally circumstances might mean that your Wirehair has to spend days, or at least part of the day, outside. If this does happen, then you will have to prepare a kennel and run for your Wirehair to use. If you intend to keep your Wirehair in a kennel all day and night, then I suggest that you reconsider actually having a dog. There is no point in purchasing a Wirehair and then committing your puppy to a lifestyle that is similar to solitary confinement. If you are still adamant that your Wirehair is to live outside, then you must consider purchasing a companion. It is not necessary for the companion to be the same breed providing that both will mature to about the same size, as they will be company for each other, and you will also overcome the problems of boredom. If you decide on a different breed, then do consider the various breeds' characteristics before finally making a decision. Purchasing two Wirehair males or a similar breed such as a large gundog, may not be a sensible idea because at some time one of your dogs will decide to make a play for the 'top dog' position. If you decide to purchase the opposite sex for your Wirehair companion you will then have to choose which one is going to be neutered to guard against an

unwanted litter. Kennels can vary in materials used, for example wood or brick, and in the overall size. If you are particularly handy in doing it yourself then the cheapest method of buying a kennel is to get a standard wooden garden shed, measuring approximately six foot by four foot. From the safety point of view, I would suggest that you build a wire-mesh frame to go over the window, both inside and outside, or replace the window with a plastic sheet. This removes any possibility of your Wirehair being hurt by coming into contact with glass. Additionally all kennels should be insulated and for this you could use a type of chipboard or plywood. To make your kennel even cosier, convert the door into a 'stable door' so that only the lower half needs to remain open and the top half will offer some protection from the elements.

If your Wirehair is only going to spend part of the day in the kennel then I would suggest that you put in either a dog bed or a doggy duvet or blanket. If you intend that your Wirehair is going to live outside permanently then you will have to prepare a bedding area. This should be constructed in the back of the kennel, away from the draughts from the window. You could also consider building a raised platform like a bench, but do not build it so far off the floor that your Wirehair puppy finds its difficult to get into, and dangerous to front legs when jumping out. Ideally it should be on floor level whilst your Wirehair puppy grows, and eventually raised to approximately six inches off the ground when your Wirehair is adult. Whichever method you decide on you must fit a retaining board on the edge to stop the type of bedding you will eventually choose from being dragged out and into the run. There are many types of bedding available from blankets, doggy duvets, straw and even shredded paper. You can also get wood shavings but we find them inclined to be very dusty and continually irritate the eyes. Whatever type you choose, remember that your Wirehair's bed will need to be changed frequently and will also need to be augmented when winter arrives.

It is very cruel to have a kennel without an attached run to enable your Wirehair to exercise freely and to keep the bed clean. The run should be well enclosed using either heavy duty galvanized chain-link fencing or weldmesh panels simply bolted into place and made tall enough to prevent escape. Providing your Wirehair has been introduced to your kennel and run at an early age the confinement will be accepted and there will be no attempts at escape. If you introduce this method of housing later on, when your Wirehair is adult, you will certainly have problems, as your Wirehair will resent it and will probably try to escape. To cope with this you would have to construct a "roof" or add to the height of the run sides with approximately twelve inches of wire turned in at the top, so that your Wirehair will not be able to climb up and over it.

For convenience we use paving slabs for the floor of the run, as this makes cleaning very simple compared to the problems associated with pebbles or grass. We also ensure that we include a raised wooden platform in the run for the Wirehair to lie on and so avoid the cold damp floor. Another point to remember if your Wirehair is destined to be a "kennel dog", is to ensure that you provide adequate shade from the sun. It is not enough for your Wirehair to have a kennel. All this means is that your Wirehair can get out of the sun but in doing so will also be denied what little breeze there may be. So, even if it is only a temporary construction, please ensure that there is a shaded area in the run all day for your Wirehair to lie in. Finally, do not think that because you have provided a run for use during either part or

It is essential to start early training and socialising as soon as your puppy arrives home.

all of the day that this will exercise your Wirehair sufficiently. Yes, your Wirehair will get a certain amount of exercise that way, but you must ensure that you provide free running exercise as well, as it is essential for health and well-being.

SOCIALISING AND TRAINING

Socialising commences immediately. This means getting your new puppy used to your way of life and giving guidance to enable your puppy to fit comfortably into your household. Understandably the puppy will be unsure of the new surroundings, having been used to just puppy quarters. During these first few hours it is best to leave the puppy to explore, offering assurance when and where necessary. Show the puppy the bed and some toys to play with. If the weather is not too cold, then you can take your Wirehair puppy outside to explore the garden. Once the new surroundings have been accepted your puppy will begin to settle and become more able to take in your teaching.

Remember you must not allow children to maul your small Wirehair puppy. You must teach children that your puppy is a living creature and is not a toy for them to play with. This does not mean that your children cannot play with your Wirehair puppy.

Puppies will soon tire after playing and will decide when it is necessary to go to bed. You must then ensure that the puppy is allowed to rest and is not disturbed by your children whilst in bed.

Wirehair puppies are naturally inquisitive and will be quick to explore their new home and garden.

HOUSE TRAINING

House training starts immediately. It is essential that after every meal or drink and always on waking up, your Wirehair puppy is taken to the part of the garden you have allocated, for toilet training outside. If you actually buy your puppy in the winter, and because of the inclement weather it is not sensible to go outside, then the training can be done on a newspaper in a specific area of your kitchen, near to your back door. I do not think it is very fair on a small puppy, who has been used to a steady room temperature, to be put outside in the howling wind and rain. In any case, your puppy would probably stand or sit by your back door shivering and would be so pleased to be allowed back into the warmth that a puddle would promptly ensue.

On the first outside excursion your puppy will probably think it is chance for play, but with time and patience will eventually realise there is more to it than that. In the early days you will probably spend a fair amount of time standing waiting for a result, so it is a good idea to give a command like "Spend a penny", or "Hurry up". Make sure that you use the same command every time and eventually your puppy will understand what to do when this command is given. You must give praise enthusiastically every time your puppy obliges, and then it will only be a question of time until complete house training has been achieved.

If accidents should happen in your home, then quickly and calmly pick the puppy up and go outside. Do not chastise a puppy for having an accident. Remember that, if you were there, you were too slow in realising what your puppy wanted to do. Additionally, during the early days, your puppy will not be able to go through the night without any accidents. Consequently it makes good sense to put some newspapers down just for the night. These can be cleaned up in the morning and you can resume the house training in the normal way.

FEEDING

The puppy's feeding should be fitted into your own routine and should take place at identical times every day. Most puppies eat readily, but don't be surprised if, in the early days, your puppy is too excited with the new surroundings to completely clear the plate of all food. Never pander to your puppy, who may well walk away from the dish before finishing it. If this happens, then pick the dish up. It will not take long before your Wirehair realises that if the dish is not cleared immediately, then both it and its contents will be removed. As I have said previously, please follow the diet sheet you were given closely, especially whilst your puppy is being given vaccinations. It is unfortunately becoming quite common to hear that puppies suffer a reaction to vaccinations. Most of these reactions are quite mild, but if they occur at the same time that you change your puppy's diet, you will not know what has caused the reaction. If the diet has been unchanged and the puppy seems to be a bit quiet after the injection, then you will know that this is not diet-related and you will need to contact your vet for further advice.

You will need to follow the diet sheet with regard to the amount of food that is to be fed at each meal. Obviously as the puppy grows it will be necessary to steadily increase the quantities of each meal. You will see by the overall condition if you are over or under feeding. If your Wirehair is well covered and is having a job to clear any meal, then you are probably being over-generous. Conversely, if your Wirehair rapidly clears the dish and looks a little on the lean side, then it is time to increase the amount. It is not a good idea to over-feed your puppy. Not only will you risk the possibilities of causing stomach upsets by creating an imbalance due to increasing the amounts of proteins and fats in excess of the amounts that are considered necessary for growth, you will also cause your puppy to become overweight, thereby affecting the growing skeletal system before it has chance to mature.

TYPES OF FOOD

There are many different types of food available these days varying from complete feeds to canned foods and even fresh food. Our puppies are reared on a complete puppy food which is, as it states, formulated to meet all the dog's nutritional requirements without the need for additives. Feeding a complete food is convenient, because you do not have to add anything, so consequently it is quick to prepare and to use. Provided you follow the manufacturers' instructions regarding quantities, a complete food will give your puppy all the necessary nutrients without causing an imbalance. This will also ensure that you do not cause your puppy to have bowel upsets due to improper feeding.

Canned foods are highly palatable and moist but nearly all of them have to be mixed with a type of biscuit to give the necessary nutritional balance. This method is not so readily used now due to the increased availability of complete feeds. It also has the drawback that as the amount of canned food and biscuit have to be mixed, there is no guarantee that the exact split is consistent for each meal. Consequently it is very easy to over-do the canned food, which will create a bowel upset, varying from a little tummy-ache to a possible visit to your vet.

Fresh food is no longer a popular method of feeding. It used to be quite easy to get scraps, mince and leftovers from the local butcher. Unfortunately, due to a decrease in the number of butchers still in business they do not seem to have great quantities of cheap leftovers available. It is still possible to buy cooked frozen tripe from some pet shops and suppliers, but for most people this is a very messy, smelly method of feeding.

No matter which method of food you finally decide to use, you must ensure that a constant supply of clean drinking water is available at all times.

VACCINATIONS

Every puppy needs to have a course of vaccinations and your vet will give you guidance as to what exactly is required. On our vet's instructions our own Wirehair puppies have a parvovirus vaccination at six weeks of age to continue the immunity given to the puppy by the mother. This means that when our Wirehair puppies are sold at seven weeks old, this vaccination has provided the initial protection and an injection will not be immediately required on arrival in the new home.

Once you have your puppy, telephone your vet and ask his advice as to when to commence the complete vaccination course. Most vets have a puppy surgery where only puppies in the process of receiving vaccinations are allowed to attend, thereby avoiding the risks involved in going to a surgery alongside ill dogs awaiting treatment. Our vet's advice is for our puppies to commence vaccinations at eight weeks with a injection covering distemper, hepatitis, leptospirosis and parvovirus. At twelve weeks our Wirehair puppies have the second part of the injection covering the same diseases. Due to the fact that we show our Wirehairs and travel around the country, our vet suggests that our Wirehair puppies have a final parvovirus injection at sixteen weeks to provide maximum protection against this serious disease.

It is important to ask your vet for advice on vaccinations, as everyone has their own ideas on when to start and on the number of injections necessary before your Wirehair is considered safe to mix with other dogs. During the course of vaccination you must remember that, until it is completed, your Wirehair puppy must be confined to your own environment and should not have contact with any other dog who is allowed outside your Wirehair's new home.

Once the vaccination course is completed, your Wirehair puppy will still have to be confined for a period of time to allow for maximum immunity to become established before you start socialising with other dogs. Do not forget that this course of vaccinations is not considered permanent; you will still need to have an annual booster to ensure that the immunity is sufficient to prevent disease.

WORMING

When you collect your Wirehair puppy it should already have completed a worming programme administered by the breeder. However it is advisable to check that this has been done. Roundworms are passed on by the mother to unborn puppies and, if worming is not done correctly, an infestation of roundworms will occur. Puppies that are severely infested will look pot-bellied, will almost certainly have diarrhoea and will not gain in weight or condition. In very serious cases of infestation death is not uncommon. Reputable breeders treat the puppies with a worming programme which starts at approximately four weeks of age. We worm our Wirehair puppies at four weeks and again at six weeks, thereby giving our puppies at least a week with us after the treatment before going to new homes. We also include the date of the last worming on each puppy's diet sheet.

The worming needs to be repeated. We suggest that on presenting your puppy to the vet for vaccination you give the date of the last worming and request that your puppy be weighed. The vet will then be able to give you the exact dose required to worm your puppy after the vaccinations are completed. Most of the modern wormers are very efficient and are convenient to use as they require no fasting. Do not combine worming with the vaccination course, as this will be very traumatic, resulting in the possibility of a very sick puppy. Worming has to be done again at six months and repeated every six months from then on for the rest of the Wirehair's life.

GROOMING

Grooming is essential and should be done on a regular basis. Daily brushing, especially after exercise, is a necessity as it will remove any grass seeds or burrs that have become embedded during exercise and will also enable you to find and treat any cuts that may have occurred. Daily grooming is also a discipline for both you and your Wirehair.

You need to start a regular grooming routine within a few days of owning your puppy. Obviously a young puppy will not be able to cope with a lengthy session, but even at seven weeks your Wirehair will not be too young to comply with this discipline. Due to the size and exuberance of your Wirehair, we always suggest that the first few grooming sessions are done up on something away from floor level. A work-top or a garden table with a towel draped across to stop your puppy from slipping is ideal. As your Wirehair will be unused to being up in the air, you should carefully hold your puppy while doing very gentle brushing. At this stage the grooming session should only last a matter of minutes. After all, there should not be too much to brush and the length of these sessions can be increased over a period of time. It might be easier to allow your Wirehair to sit during these initial sessions, and this will, provided you give the instruction "Sit", teach this command.

Remember that grooming is a discipline and no matter how young your puppy is you need to start instilling obedience immediately. You must decide when the grooming session is finished, not the puppy. If there is any struggling, then you should insist that the puppy remains being groomed for a few moments more before you give the signal for release. If your Wirehair resents being restrained and starts to show displeasure by biting, then this trait must be stopped immediately with a sharp tap on the nose with your finger combined with the command "No". As your Wirehair grows, you should introduce the command "Stand" because this position is more convenient for grooming than sitting. Once you are sure your Wirehair is reasonably obedient and will either sit or stand to be groomed, then you can

Ch. Bareve Bramble: Good diet and regular exercise are the key to rearing a healthy dog.

John Hartley

A grooming pad and a comb is all you need for everyday grooming.

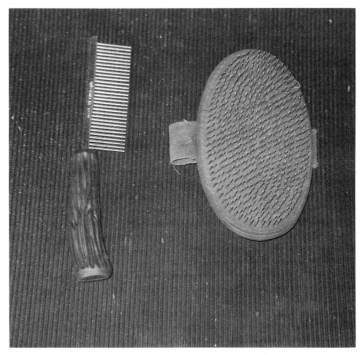

continue at floor level. For brushing we use a wire grooming pad and a comb. A wire grooming pad is a small oval rubber backed pad with a strap, the face of which is covered with wire teeth approximately one centimetre long. We also use a traditional comb with a handle for comfortable use. The grooming pad will remove any dead undercoat together with any dirt that has accumulated in the double coat of the Wirehair. The comb is used to comb the face whiskers to prevent any tangles from appearing. By the time your Wirehair is able to be taken out for daily exercise, you should be receiving a reasonable amount of obedience and the grooming procedure should be done without any resistance.

When you have reached the stage where your Wirehair will be brushed without any problems, you need to extend the procedure to include other items, for example checking teeth, ears and nails.

TEETH

Teeth should be checked on a weekly basis and initially this will amount to no more than a quick look to check the cleanliness. Some people actually clean their dog's teeth with special dog toothpaste, others rely on uncooked marrow bones to help with dental cleansing. We clean and scale our own Wirehairs' teeth with a canine dental scaler, but this requires absolute obedience and should not be considered unless you are confident about your own Wirehair's steadiness. The safest suggestion for removing any build-up of tartar is for your vet to do this under a light anaesthetic if it is considered necessary. There again, even if there is nothing or very little you need to do when you check your dog's teeth, it is still a discipline that your Wirehair must comply with.

NAILS

Nails need to be checked and it is advisable to do this every day. It seems that the feet of Wirehairs are very sensitive, as it is surprising how many really hate having this done. Consequently I would suggest that you pick each foot up in turn and hold it for a few moments, checking the nails daily from quite an early age. Do not forget that most breeders do not remove the dewclaws, so see if your puppy has any and if so remember to check those at the same time as the other nails. Once your Wirehair starts to go out for regular walks you will probably have to cut your dog's nails less frequently. It is during the period of joining the new household and being old enough to go out that the nails will probably have to be trimmed. After all, the only surfaces your Wirehair puppy will have access to will be your carpets and the grass in your garden. Neither will keep the nails at a reasonable length. A good investment would be a guillotine nail-cutter which would enable you to keep the nails tidy without the need to visit the vet. When cutting your dog's nails care must be taken because the nail is dark, so you will be unable to see where the quick ends. It is best if you just cut the oversharp tip of the nail. If you cut into the quick or if your Wirehair damages a nail whilst exercising, causing the nail to bleed, apply permanganate of potash and this will stop the bleeding.

EARS

Ears also need regular checking and cleaning, and because the ears are delicate, great care must be taken. Initially you should ensure that your puppy will allow you to gently clean the inside of the ear flap with a tissue, even if it comes away unmarked. If the tissue shows some ear grease, then take another tissue and continue until the ear flap is clean. Unfortunately the Wirehair grows thin wispy hair down the ear canal and, to prevent possible ear infections and problems, this hair needs to be removed. We actually use a pair of round-ended tweezers to remove this hair but, as I have said earlier with regard to the scaling of teeth, you need absolute obedience. You can also pluck this hair out by hand, especially if you rub some chalk on to your fingers to help establish a grip.

You need to get your Wirehair to lie down flat on one side and to stay in that position whilst you are removing the hair. If your Wirehair has very heavy hair-growth inside the ear canal, then remove the hair bit by bit, or you could make the ear very sore and your dog will not be so co-operative the next time you want to remove the hairs. You must teach your puppy from an early age to lie down flat and remain there so that you can do the´ear inspection. This is essential whether you are able to cope with the hair removal yourself or whether you want your vet to do it, because it will make his job easier and it can be done without the need for an anaesthetic.

If, in spite of all the preventative ear care, your Wirehair starts scratching them determinedly and, on inspection, the ear canal looks inflamed and smells bad, then I would suggest a visit to your vet who will be able to suggest the correct course of treatment. It is also common for puppies who are teething to scratch around the ears. This seems to be in an effort to try and relieve the discomfort of the swollen and painful gums. Provided that on inspection the ears do not look inflamed or smell, then you can relax and ignore this behaviour.

I would suggest that you do your grooming procedure after the daily exercise, as your Wirehair will be tired and more likely to co-operate fully. Give a complete brushing and include the checking of eyes, ears, feet and above the elbow in the equivalent of arm pits for any foreign bodies such as grass seed. It does not take long for either an untreated cut to cause problems or a grass seed to work into the skin and fester, causing an abscess to form, so this detailed grooming could save you a lot of heartbreak and an expensive veterinary bill.

EXERCISE

All exercise should be confined to your garden until your Wirehair has successfully completed the course of vaccinations. Why take unnecessary risks in exercising over ground that other dogs use and for a matter of the few weeks until your puppy has secured protection from disease. At such a young age the routine is simply play for a short while, sleep for a while, then wake up and continue playing. Too much exercise at this stage will cause permanent damage to a growing puppy's frame.

You can take advantage of this period to do some training with a collar and lead. It is too traumatic to expose your Wirehair to the big outside world while experiencing walking on a collar and lead for the first time. It is better to buy a small collar and to put that on loosely, before you consider attaching a lead to it. The first reaction will be to scratch and try to remove it, or to shake vigorously to try and dislodge it, but after a relatively short while the puppy will become accustomed to it. To assist acclimatisation, it is also a good idea to use the collar during grooming as a means of restraint while you teach the necessary commands of Sit, Stand and Down. Leave the collar on for increasingly long periods during the day but never leave it on at night or when your puppy is left unsupervised.

After a while, when there is no longer any objection to pressure being put on to the collar, you can consider attaching a lead to it. There are several methods of teaching a dog to walk on a lead. Whichever method you use you must remember to give a lot of encouragement and not to make the lessons so long that the pupil will become resentful.

I do not take our Wirehair puppies for long walks until they are at least six months old. The best exercise for growing puppies is to have free running, but this must be monitored carefully so that when your puppy starts to tire, then you can stop it. If you fail to do this, there is a great risk of incurring injury.

Steadily increase the amount of free running exercise as your Wirehair matures and finds it easier to cope with. The adult Wirehair has unlimited energy, relishes exercise and will take as much working and free running as you can give. One point of caution: during the summer it is advisable that exercise is done early in the morning and late at night, when it is considerably cooler. No dogs should be forced to exercise during the hottest part of the day.

Chapter Four

THE IMPORTANCE OF TRAINING

It is clearly the duty of responsible owners to ensure that their dog is given adequate training as a puppy and does not become a menace to our society. Remember that every dog is a reflection of the owner and if your Wirehair becomes a nuisance, an uncontrollable spoilt brat, then this will also reflect on the breed as a whole. Alternatively a well-behaved, happy, pleasant Wirehair will create a good impression on everyone and will do a very successful PR job for the breed. Whatever your ambitions are with your Wirehair, you will need basic Obedience and control at all times. There must be discipline and firmness, but never be cruel or brutal. The Wirehair is a very intelligent breed – combined with a little stubbornness – and therefore needs consistent, fair and firm guidance throughout life.

TRAINING METHODS
Methods of training vary considerably. Whichever method you decide to try, you must always remain calm and confident. Never lose your temper and administer unjust punishment. Remember to give lavish praise every time your commands are correctly completed. The art behind Obedience training is repetition, but guard against prolonging your exercises and thereby making your Wirehair bored.

A piece of advice that we were given by Mieneke Mills de Hoog when we bought our first Wirehair was most valuable. We were told always to remember to ask for something to be done once and, if it was not done straightaway, the request was to be repeated and we were to insist that it was carried out. Most people who experience problems with disobedient Wirehairs are those who have not insisted on commands being obeyed. It is all too easy to command a young Wirehair puppy to sit, and to be confronted with an appealing, whiskery face coupled with a naughty expression pleading with you not to insist on your command. But if you do not detach yourself from this pleading and insist on your command being obeyed, you will have laid the first foundations of disobedience. The Wirehair has the intelligence to 'test the system' and having been allowed to get away with something will build on this continually.

Remember that dogs in general are pack animals with a well-defined social order, and through all basic training you must become the pack leader. As I have said before, you must not be cruel, because a Wirehair can be very sensitive and responds better to the different tones of your voice than to any physical remonstrations.

Ch. Bareve Bramble demonstrating a correctly fitting check chain.

TYPES OF COMMANDS

The tone of your voice is of the utmost importance and you will have to ensure that all the nice words of praise and command are given in a pleasant, happy tone and all the No and Stop commands are said in a disapproving tone. Dogs do not understand long sentences, so your commands need to be short and simple combined with the relevant tone of voice. Men seem to have more problems with this than women, as their voices are lower. Therefore men will need to work at lifting their voices for the nice commands and the subsequent praise. You must also be consistent. Dogs need to be given the same command for the same action, preceded with their name. It is no good expecting a dog to sit every time if you say "Ben, Sit" one time and then another time say "Ben, go and sit down".

For basic Obedience the commands I would suggest you teach are No, Sit, Down, Stand, Stay, Heel and Come. For No, Down, and Stay, I would speak in a low voice; Stand would be in a slightly higher tone. The Sit command would be given in a normal voice tone but with emphasis on the S and the T. The Heel command would also be given in a normal voice tone, but the Come command would be given in a higher, upbeat tone. After all, you want your Wirehair to come to you, so make sure that this command actually gives the

Ch. Bareve Bramble sitting at heel, looking up to her handler for the next command.

impression of encouragement. Do remember that all commands need to be preceded with your Wirehair's name, because this is the way you will initially gain attention.

COMING WHEN CALLED

All the basic commands are best taught in the safe, familiar surroundings of your garden. Right from day one you should be using your puppy's name together with the command Come every time you want your puppy to come to you. Until you get a response to that command you cannot really progress to the others.

In the first stages try not to give the command when your puppy is running around playing, but wait until there is no distraction and then call your puppy's name together with the instruction "Come". Then kneel down with your arms outstretched ready to welcome your puppy with great words of praise. The average puppy enjoys freedom and will resent being made to surrender it. Try to counteract this problem by not restraining your Wirehair every time the Come command is obeyed. Just make a fuss, give lots of praise and then set the puppy free again. In no time the realisation will dawn that obeying the command does not always mean that freedom has come to an end.

If, after a while, your puppy becomes complacent on being called and refuses to come immediately, you should ignore this disobedience and walk away, preferably out of sight. Natural curiosity, combined with the sudden feeling of isolation, will ensure that your puppy comes to look for you. Respond with praise and affection when you are found but do not make the mistake of restricting your puppy. Allow freedom again almost immediately. The next time you give the command Come your puppy should respond properly.

Never scold a puppy for not coming straight back, because the wrong connections will be made. The puppy will connect the scolding with coming back to the owner, rather than with the previous action, which was that of not coming properly when called. You will then have the absolute opposite effect from the one you wished to achieve. Also never let any exercise become so protracted that your Wirehair becomes bored. Stop before you get to that point, and always remember to stop on a good note.

WALKING AT HEEL

Hopefully, the first time your puppy can go for a walk, the art of coping with a collar and lead will have been mastered. Always have your Wirehair on the lefthand side, as this is the most usual side to teach your dog to walk at heel. The only exception to this is people who wish to work their Wirehair with Falcons. The left hand is always used to carry and transport the Falcons, so it is advisable to teach your Wirehair to walk on the righthand side from the outset.

Once your puppy is accustomed to walking on a collar and lead, and before any detailed Obedience work is considered, you should introduce a suitable slip chain. You must remember that when your Wirehair is fully mature, you will have quite a large and powerful dog on the end of a lead. Collars are useful when teaching a puppy to walk on a lead; however, I do not think that any adult Wirehair should be walked or worked on one. All of our dogs and bitches are introduced to a slip chain between three and four months of age, and are always worked in one from then on.

No Wirehair, whether a young dog or an old one, should be allowed to pull on the lead, so teaching a dog to walk to heel is very important. So start with your Wirehair, wearing a slip chain collar, on the lefthand side, with the lead in your right hand. Gain attention by calling your dog's name followed with the command "Heel" and step off with your left foot. If it is necessary to encourage the dog forward when you step off, then either pat your left leg with your left hand at the same time or give a short jerk on the lead. It is most unlikely that any dog will refuse to move off, so as soon as your dog responds, remember to give lots of praise and keep moving forward, encouraging your dog as you go.

Try not to have the lead constantly tight, as this will not teach your Wirehair anything, other than how to pull and lean into the chain. Conversely a loose lead, allowing meandering, will also be a waste of time. The ideal is to have the lead short enough, allowing the slip chain to be fairly loose, so that if your Wirehair starts to walk in front, the chain will tighten. If this happens remind your puppy to "Heel", simultaneously giving a short jerk on the lead, which allows the slip chain to loosen again. At no point should you actually stop moving forward. Obviously it is not always convenient to walk in straight lines, so you will have to teach your Wirehair to remain at heel whenever you change

The first stage of a Sit-Stay, on lead.

Ch. Bareve Bramble successfully completing a Stand-Stay, off lead.

A combined family Down-Stay. Pictured left to right: Bareve Brocade, Ch. Bareve Bramble, Bareve Beinn Eighe, Ch. Bareve Frau Holle and Matilde Renata.

direction. Provided that you call your Wirehair's name combined with the command Heel each time you change direction, then in no time at all your Wirehair will be constantly walking to heel.

Even if you do not wish to compete in Obedience competitions, it is a good exercise to incorporate sitting whenever you come to a halt. When you halt, have the lead in your right hand, command your Wirehair to Sit, raise your right hand and give the lead a short backward jerk; at exactly the same time use your left hand to push the hindquarters down. Do not wait too long for minds to be made up. If there is any hint that your Wirehair is not going to react immediately, then you must enforce the sitting position. This will encourage your puppy to do it quickly.

TRAINING CLASSES

Once your Wirehair has learned to obey these simple commands, then I would advise you to enrol in a local Obedience class. These are relatively inexpensive and are ideal for teaching sociability with other dogs and their owners. Even if you are considering showing your Wirehair, successfully completing a beginners course in Obedience will do no harm at all. Even at shows you still need to have an obedient dog and one who will mix and behave well with other canine company. All you need to do when enrolling is to inform the instructor that you are considering showing your puppy, and so on some occasions, instead of sitting at the halt, you can teach your puppy to stand. Most of our Wirehairs have done at least a beginners course in Obedience and we have successfully combined the different halts.

One of the next exercises to be introduced is the Down command. Ideally the best way to start is when your puppy is already lying down (not asleep), and actually say "Down". If your Wirehair is already sitting, then you need to give the command "Down" and with your right hand on your puppy's chest push gently backwards and, at the same time, with your left hand on the point of the shoulders push firmly downwards. This combination should produce the down position. Again, remember great praise when your Wirehair actually completes the exercise.

The other important exercise is Stay. Use whichever position your dog is more comfortable doing, either the sitting or the down position. Initially with your Wirehair at heel you must give the command Stay and leave your dog, leading with your right leg. Now, you are wondering why you have to lead with your other leg. I was taught a long time ago that if I was doing an exercise that required my dog to go with me I was to step off using my left leg. After all, this is the leg that is nearest the dog when sitting at heel. However, if I was doing an exercise which meant that my dog had to wait until either I returned or I gave a different command, I had to step off with my right leg – that is, the leg which is furthest away from the dog at heel.

Your first Stays should be very short as the object of the exercise is to get your Wirehair to remain in position and for you to return before there is any movement. If during these early exercises you think your Wirehair is going to move, do not be afraid to repeat the command frequently. Try to anticipate your dog's actions. It is a lot easier to repeat the command than to have to start the whole exercise again. Obviously, increase the time and distance whenever you consider that your Wirehair is capable of successfully completing the exercise. If there is any doubt about steadiness, then stick to the same time and distance until you are sure.

TRAVELLING BY CAR

In most cases the longest journey a puppy will undertake in early life is the journey from the breeder to the new home. I have said previously that it is important to make the initial car journey as comfortable as you can so that your Wirehair comes to enjoy the car and does not fear and hate travelling. Gradually introduce your car and subsequent journeys. Start by putting your puppy into the car whilst it is stationary, and then build up to short journeys. If your Wirehair is still unsettled by the car then I suggest that you drive to a destination where there are good walks and opportunities for games. This should overcome any problems, when your Wirehair realises that at the end of a journey there is something really enjoyable.

Do not allow your Wirehair to jump straight out of the car as soon as the door is open. This is another part of training when you can insist that your dog learns to stay. Give the command Stay as soon as the door is open, even if some initial restraint is necessary until the lesson has been learned.

JUMPING UP

Another problem you might have to deal with is if your Wirehair keeps jumping up at people. You must try to anticipate when this is going to happen and stop it. If your Wirehair does jump up, then you must give the command "No" and actually place the puppy's legs back down on the floor. As soon as you have done this, you must make a great fuss of your puppy in that position. By doing this, you will have shown you dislike the jumping up and are praising the return to the floor. If you have allowed your Wirehair to jump up and then, as your puppy grows, you realise it has not been a good idea to allow this to occur, then you might have to resort to squeezing your Wirehair's feet at the same time as saying "No".

Once you have completed a beginners class in Obedience you should then know what you and your Wirehair want to do. Even if you do not progress onto the next Obedience class or actually commence either a Field Trial or show career, at least what you and your Wirehair will have learned by this stage will help you to enjoy your lives together.

Chapter Five

THE BREED STANDARDS

The Breed Standard is a description of the ideal specimen of the breed. It is a guide that breeders use in their efforts to breed quality Wirehairs and it is the means by which judges evaluate the dogs in the show ring and it helps them reach their final decisions. It gives exact details of every feature of the Wirehair including physical make-up and temperament and describes the characteristics that make this breed different from other dogs.

There are three main Standards for the German Wirehaired Pointer: the German, the American, and the English Standard.

THE GERMAN BREED STANDARD

GENERAL APPEARANCE
Pointer of noble appearance, hard hair that covers all of the skin, lively temperament, attentive, energetic facial expressions. Movements should be powerful, spacious, fluent and harmonic. Colours dark to middle brown, brown/roan, brown/white also black/roan with or without spots.

HEAD AND MOUTH
Head should be in proportion with body size and sex with a long, broad, powerful mouth. Complete, powerful teeth. No overhanging skin. Medium sized high broad cheeks. Clear preferably dark eyes. Eyelids closing well.

BODY
Chest should be broad and deep with clear forechest and a breast bone that carries well backward. Ribs well curved back. Back should be short with a straight only lightly sloping backline. Muscles on thighs. Hips should be broad.
Croup – Long, broad, lightly sloping, well muscled.
Withers – erected, long, well muscled.
Stomach – lightly raised to the back.
Loins – short.

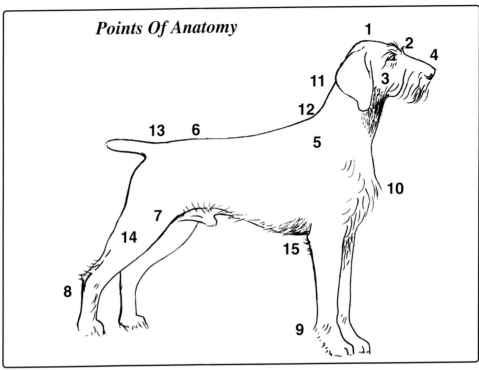

Points Of Anatomy

1. Skull	6. Loin	11. Neck
2. Stop	7. Stifle	12. Withers
3. Cheek	8. Hock	13. Tail set
4. Muzzle	9. Pastern	14. Second thigh
5. Shoulder	10. Brisket	15. Elbow

FRONT AND BACK LIMBS

Shoulder – good fitting into body and slanting. Upper arm as long as possible.

Elbows – not pointed outside or bent.

Legs – strong, sharp, vertical towards ground, movement supporting angle of the back legs.

Paws – oval with closed toes and thick coarse balls of the feet.

TAIL

Shortened following the backline in direction. If possible horizontal or slightly upward.

SKIN

Tightly clinging without folds or creases.

*Sh. Ch. Bareve
Baton Rouge,
pictured in the
UK, 1990.*

David Bull.

HAIR
Wirehaired, hard, clinging, thick top coat – cover hair two to four centimetres long.
Undercoat thick. Outline of the body should not be hidden through a coat that is too
long. Should give good protection through its hardness and thickness against weather
and injuries.
Under-body and legs short, but well covered – top of body and head somewhat thicker
but not softer.
Visible eyebrows; strong but not too long but if possible hard beard.
SIZE
Males – 61/68 cms.
Females – 57/64 cms.
Supplied by the Verein Deutsch-Drahthaar (and translated as near to verbatim as possible).

THE AMERICAN BREED STANDARD

GENERAL APPEARANCE
The German Wirehaired Pointer is a well muscled, medium sized dog of distinctive
appearance. Balanced in size and sturdily built, the breed's most distinguishing
characteristics are its weather-resistant, wire-like coat and its facial furnishings.
Typically pointer in character and style, the German Wirehaired Pointer is an
intelligent, energetic and determined hunter.

SIZE, PROPORTION, SUBSTANCE

The height of males should be from twenty-four to twenty-six inches at the withers. Bitches are smaller but not under twenty-two inches. To insure the working quality of the breed is maintained, dogs that are either over or under the specified height must be severely penalized. The body is a little longer than it is high, as ten is to nine. The German Wirehaired Pointer is a versatile hunter built for agility and endurance in the field. Correct size and balance are essential to high performance.

HEAD

The head is moderately long. Eyes are brown, medium in size, oval in contour, bright and clear and overhung with medium length eyebrows. Yellow eyes are not desirable. The ears are rounded but not too broad and hang close to the head.

The skull broad and the occipital bone not too prominent. The stop is medium. The muzzle is fairly long with nasal bone straight, broad and parallel to the top of the skull. The nose is dark brown with nostrils wide open. A spotted or flesh colored nose is to be penalized. The lips are a trifle pendulous but close to the jaw and bearded. The jaws are strong with a full complement of evenly set and properly intermeshing teeth. The incisors meet in a true scissors bite.

NECK, TOPLINE, BODY

The neck is of medium length, slightly arched and devoid of dewlap. The entire back line showing a perceptible slope down from withers to croup. The skin throughout is notably tight to the body. The chest is deep and capacious with ribs well sprung. The tuck-up apparent. The back is short, straight and strong. Loins are taut and slender. Hips are broad with the croup nicely rounded. The tail is set high, carried at or above the horizontal when the dog is alert. The tail is docked to approximately two-fifths of its original length.

FOREQUARTERS

The shoulders are well laid back. The forelegs are straight with elbows close. Leg bones are flat rather than round, and strong, but not so heavy or coarse as to militate against the dog's natural agility. Dewclaws are generally removed. Round in outline, the feet are webbed, high arched with toes close, pads thick and hard, and nails strong and quite heavy.

HINDQUARTERS

The angulation of the highquarters balances that of the forequarters. The thighs are strong and muscular. The hind legs are moderately angulated at the stifle and hock and, as viewed from behind, parallel to each other. Dewclaws are generally removed. Feet as in front.

COAT

The functional wiry coat is the breed's most distinctive feature. A dog must have a correct coat to be of correct type. The coat is weather resistant and, to some extent, water repellant. The undercoat is dense enough in winter to insulate against the cold but is so thin in summer as to be almost invisible. The distinctive outer coat is straight, harsh, wiry and flat lying, and is from one to two inches in length. The outer coat is long enough to protect against the punishment of rough cover, but not so long as to hide the outline of the dog. On the lower legs the coat is shorter and between the toes it is of softer texture. On the skull the coat is naturally short and close fitting. Over the shoulders and round the tail it is very dense and heavy. The tail is nicely coated, particularly on the underside, but devoid of feather. Eyebrows are of strong, straight hair. Beard and whiskers are medium length. The hairs in the liver patches of a liver and white dog may be shorter than the white hairs. A short smooth coat, a soft woolly coat, or an excessively long coat is to be severely penalized. While maintaining a harsh, wiry texture, the puppy coat may be shorter than that of an adult coat. Coats may be neatly groomed to present a dog natural in appearance. Extreme and excessive grooming to present a dog artificial in appearance should be severely penalized.

COLOR
The coat is liver and white, usually either liver and white spotted, liver roan, liver and white spotted with ticking and roaning or solid liver. The head is liver, sometimes with a white blaze. The ears are liver. Any black in the coat is to be severely penalized.

GAIT
The dog should be evaluated at a moderate gait. The movement is free and smooth with good reach in the forequarters and good driving power in the hindquarters. The topline should remain firm.

TEMPERAMENT
Of sound reliable temperament, the German Wirehaired Pointer is at times aloof but not unfriendly towards strangers: a loyal and affectionate companion who is eager to please and enthusiastic to learn.
Approved by the AKC July 9 1985, reformatted May 14, 1989. Reproduced with permission of the AKC.

THE ENGLISH BREED STANDARD

GENERAL APPEARANCE
Medium sized hunting dog with wire hair completely covering skin. Overall should be slightly longer in body, compared to shoulder height.

CHARACTERISTICS
Powerful, strong, versatile hunting dog, excels in both field and water. Loyal, intelligent, sound temperament and alert.

TEMPERAMENT
Gentle, affectionate and even-tempered. Alert, biddable and very loyal.

HEAD AND SKULL
Balanced in proportion to body. Skull sufficiently broad and slightly rounded. Moderate stop, skull and muzzle of equal length with no overhanging lips. Nose liver or black.

EYES
Medium sized oval, hazel or darker, with eyelids closing properly, not protruding nor too deep set.

EARS
Medium sized in relation to head, set high, when brought forward should reach corner of lips.

MOUTH
Teeth and jaws strong, with perfect regular and complete scissor bite, i.e. upper teeth closely overlapping lower teeth and set square to the jaws, with full dentition.

NECK
Strong and of adequate length, skin tightly fitting.

FOREQUARTERS
Shoulders sloping and very muscular with top of shoulder blades not too close; upper arm bones between shoulder and elbow long. Elbows close to body, neither pointing outwards nor inwards. Forelegs straight and lean, sufficiently muscular and strong but not coarse-boned. Pasterns slightly sloping, almost straight but not quite.

BODY
Chest must appear deep rather than wide but not out of proportion to the rest of the body; ribs deep and well sprung, never barrel-shaped nor flat, back ribs reaching well down to tucked up loins. Chest measurement immediately behind elbows smaller than that of about a hand's-breadth behind elbows so that upper arm has freedom of movement. Firm back, not arched, with slightly falling back line.

HINDQUARTERS
Hips broad and wide, croup falling slightly towards tail. Thighs strong and well muscled. Stifles well bent. Hock square with body, turning neither in nor out. Pasterns nearly upright. Bone strong but not coarse.

FEET
Compact, close-knit, round to oval shaped, well padded, should turn neither in nor out. Toes well arched, heavily nailed.

GAIT/MOVEMENT
Smooth, covering plenty of ground with each stride, driving hind action, elbows neither in nor out. Definitely not a hackney action.

TAIL
Starts high and thick, growing gradually thinner. Customarily docked to approximately two-fifths of original length. When quiet, tail should be carried down, when moving, horizontally, never held high over back or bent. Tail set following continuation of back line.

COAT
Outer coat thicker and harsh, no longer than 3.8 cms (1 1/2 ins) long with a dense under coat (under coat more prevalent in winter than summer). It should not hide body shape but it should be long enough to give good protection. Coat should lie close to the body. Hair on head and ears thick and short, but not too soft. Bushy eyebrows, full but not overlong beard.

COLOUR
Liver and white, solid liver, black and white. Solid black and tri-coloured highly undesirable.

SIZE
Ideal height at shoulder: Dogs: 60–67 cms (24–26 ins). Bitches: 56–62 cms (22–24 ins) Weight: Dogs: 25–34 kgs (55–75 lbs). Bitches: 20 1/2–29 kgs (45–64 lbs).

FAULTS
Any departure from the foregoing points should be considered a fault and the seriousness with which the fault should be regarded should be in exact proportion to its degree.

NOTE: Male animals should have two apparently normal testicles fully descended into the scrotum.
Reproduced by kind permission of the English Kennel Club.

INTERPRETATION

GENERAL APPEARANCE, CHARACTERISTICS
It is difficult to make comparisons between the different Standards as the English Standard is far more condensed than the other versions. However, all the Standards agree that the Wirehair should be a medium-sized dog that is capable of hunting and working. The Standards actually make the point that Wirehairs are intelligent and are energetic, powerful and determined hunters. Even if you do not work your Wirehair these statements accurately describe the natural characteristics of the Wirehair, giving a true impression of the unlimited

Ch. Jamars Oh Henry showing a typical head and expression with the correct medium length of beard and eyebrows.

ability of the breed. Additionally, mention is made of the essential weather-resistant wire coat, one of the breed's most important features. The English Standard actually mentions, as part of the general appearance, the other most important feature, the essential height to length proportions. It is essential that people realise that the Wirehair must not be short in body length. The Wirehair is not a wire-coated German Shorthair Pointer. Please study the diagrams and note the difference in overall shape!

TEMPERAMENT

No matter how good a specimen your Wirehair is, there is no room in our society for dogs of questionable temperament. Most Wirehairs will have to mix with people, children and other dogs, so any sign of unstable temperament should be greatly frowned upon and not be allowed to escalate through breeding with those Wirehairs.

The Wirehair should be affectionate, even-tempered and certainly very loyal. I feel that it was a great shame that the English Kennel Club, at the time of streamlining the Standards, left out the statement 'aloof with strangers'. A good percentage of Wirehairs, although very affectionate, are somewhat aloof with people they do not know. On the other hand, I do not agree with the statement about being gentle, as this gives the impression of calm and steadiness. If you live with a normal Wirehair you will soon realise that the word 'gentle' does not apply. Wirehairs are not a very fizzy breed, but when excited you do realise what a powerful dog you have got.

HEAD

All Standards describe a similar type of head – moderately long, but with skull and muzzle of equal length and balanced in relation with the whole of the dog. After all, the Wirehair must be capable of having the power in its jaws to carry large game.

EYES

The same medium oval-shaped eye is required, preferably hazel or brown. Eye colour does change with age. A six month old puppy will not have particularly dark eyes but during the maturing process the eye colour will keep darkening. Not every Wirehair will finish with a good eye colour and it would seem that those that have light coloured eyes in adulthood stem from particular broodlines.

EARS

There seems little variance in the Standards with regard to the overall size and placement of the ears.

MOUTH

All Standards require the mouth to be of a scissor bite. In England judges normally check just the bite to ensure that it is a scissor bite. On occasions when we have had German judges over to officiate at our shows, they have always been more thorough and will usually check and count the number of teeth each dog has. But, please note that it is not uncommon for the number one premolars on the bottom jaw in young Wirehairs to be very slow in coming through. We had a Wirehair bitch that had all the lower incisors missing right up until she was six months old. Yet by the time she was eight months old, all six teeth were through and were straight, resulting in a correct scissor bite. So please be patient where teeth are concerned and do not be tempted to make hasty decisions.

NECK AND BODY

The American Standard asks for a slightly arched neck and, to me, that just puts the

DENTITION

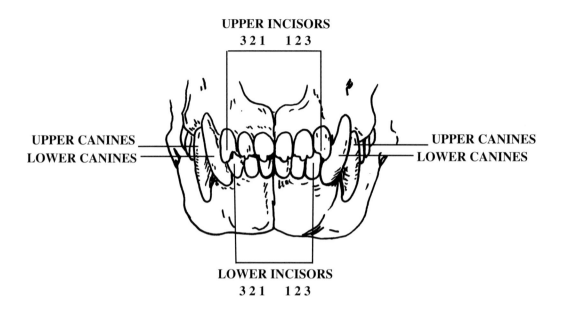

UPPER INCISORS
3 2 1   1 2 3

UPPER CANINES
LOWER CANINES

UPPER CANINES
LOWER CANINES

LOWER INCISORS
3 2 1   1 2 3

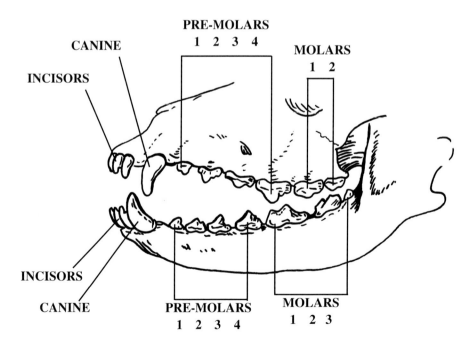

PRE-MOLARS
1 2 3 4

MOLARS
1 2

CANINE

INCISORS

INCISORS

CANINE

PRE-MOLARS
1 2 3 4

MOLARS
1 2 3

EXAMPLES OF BITES

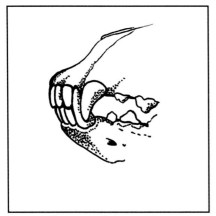

Correct: Scissor bite.

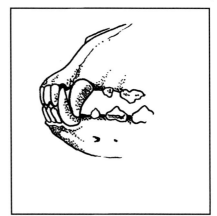

Incorrect: Level bite.

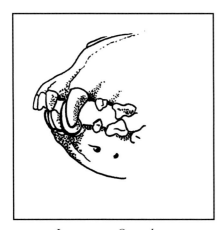

Incorrect: Overshot.

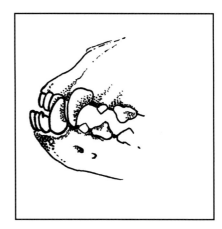

Incorrect: Undershot.

finishing touch to a good length of neck. As the breed is a working gundog, we do need a reasonable length of neck to enable the Wirehair to get down and pick up its game. Fortunately the breed does not suffer from having excessive dewlap.

The English and American Standards require the breed to be longer in body than in height. However, the English Standard calls for a firm back, while the American and German Standards state that the back is to be short. On this point I prefer the English version, because most people seem to think that a short back means a dog that is short in body.

As you can see by the diagrams, you can have a dog that is longer in body than in height and still have a relatively short, firm back. Yet with a dog that measures the same length and

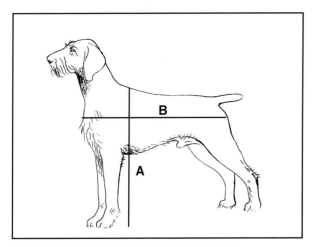

Correct proportions for a Wirehair: A:B equals 9:10. A dog that is 26ins high should be approximately 28.5ins long in body.

Correct proportions for a German Shorthaired Pointer: A:B:10:10. A dog that is 25ins high should be 25ins long in body.

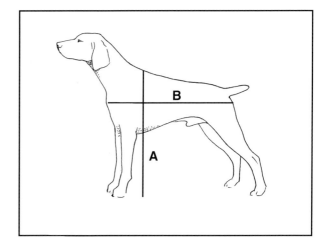

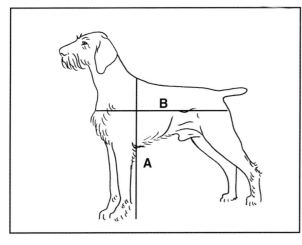

Incorrect Proportions for a Wirehair:A:B are equal, consequently this Wirehair is too short.

height, giving a square appearance, the actually length of back is shorter still.

The English Standard asks for the back not to be arched, with a slightly falling back line, along with the American Standard and German Standard asking for a slight sloping from withers to croup. A new problem in the Wirehair in Britain is when dogs that are considered too short in body actually have a roached topline. This is ugly, and I sincerely hope that Wirehairs with this serious structural fault will not be used as breeding stock.

FOREQUARTERS AND HINDQUARTERS

Again, the Standards do not really vary much. I do like the American statement that "The angulation of the hindquarter balances that of the forequarters." How many times do we see Wirehairs that are upright in shoulder being similarly upright in the hindquarters? In the American Standard there is no mention of the correct angle of the pasterns, whereas the English Standard asks for slightly sloping pasterns, almost straight but not quite.

Another point is that the American Standard states that the dewclaws are generally removed. This is rarely done in England, as our German breeder friends insist that these are left on. When the Wirehairs are being assessed by a German judge he will actually look for them and penalise the dog if they have been removed. It is also unfortunate that the English Standard has left out the fact that the Wirehair feet are webbed.

Two examples of hindquarters: On the left the dog has good, straight, short hocks; on the right the dog is cow-hocked.

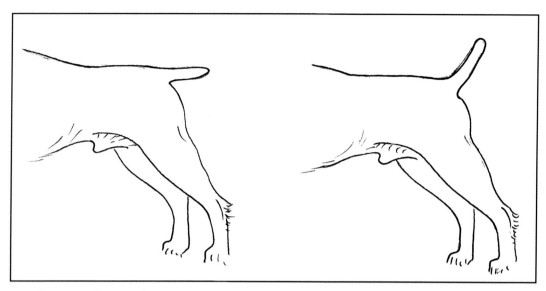

Correct tail-set and carriage.   *Incorrect: tail carriage is too high.*

TAIL

All Standards ask for the tail to be docked to two-fifths of its original length. Legislation has been introduced in Britain making it illegal for lay people to dock puppies' tails. It can only be done by authorised veterinary surgeons. However, in 1992 the Royal College of Veterinary Surgeons ruled that all docking is unethical "unless for therapeutic or acceptable prophylactic reasons". The RCVS, who have campaigned for this decision, listed the circumstances in which they consider prophylactic docking to be acceptable. These now make the routine docking of puppies by vets extremely difficult. The RCVS have gone on to say that those vets who continue to dock could risk disciplinary action, including being struck off the professional register.

In view of the possible implications for both breeders and vets, it now looks as though British breeders are going to have great difficulty finding vets who will continue docking. Now the Council of Docked Breeds has been formed. Two of their aims are to promote and maintain the right of vets to continue docking and to promote the need for a docking register permitting trained non-veterinaries to dock puppies. If they succeed with either of them, it will help British breeders who, in the present situation, are going to find docking very difficult to achieve.

I consider it is necessary to continue docking Wirehairs' tails to avoid damage. Even if you do not actually work your Wirehair, the natural hunting ability which comes to the fore when exercising could result in the tail end being ripped, causing severe bleeding. This type of tail-end laceration is extremely painful and most difficult to treat successfully.

Regarding tail carriage, the American Standard allows the tail to be carried at or above the horizontal when the dog is alert. I feel that the British Standard, which requires the tail never to be held high over the back, or bent, is more desirable. The very high set tail being carried at almost 90 degrees to the back is an ugly sight, completely detracting from the impression of a Pointer. These tails are much better suited to the Terrier breeds.

Just take time to consider: a high-flying docked tail is bad enough but what would be the effect of a full tail? I rather think that sooner or later we shall have Wirehairs being shown with tails resembling Foxhounds in full flight.

COAT

I feel that, along with the correct body proportions, correct coat is of prime importance and is one of the main breed features. The American Standard states that "a dog must have a correct coat to be of correct type," and actually gives a very explicit description of what is deemed to be a correct coat.

In the show ring I do not think enough importance is attached to a Wirehair's coat. It is very common to read show reports, knowing the individual exhibits in question, and to realise the vast differences in judges' opinions in their evaluations of coat quality. Wirehairs with long, open coats devoid of undercoat but with heavy facial whiskers are placed over Wirehairs with a slightly shorter length of coat, with correct undercoat and maybe fewer whiskers on the face. This is totally incorrect.

Please note that the main reason for the wire coat is that it provides protection against hunting injuries and all weather elements and is, virtually, a waterproof coat when swimming. This means that you need the outer coat to be as flat as possible, with dense

Bareve Brunhilde illustrating correct coat type and texture.

David Dalton.

An incorrect coat: This bitch's coat is not a typical 'woolly coat' because, although it is a heavy open coat that is not lying flat, it is of a reasonable texture and it has retained its rich colours.

undercoat giving the required protection. Outer coat that can be seen blowing in the wind is obviously not lying close, so it cannot offer protection. The outer coat must feel hard and wiry to the touch when you place the flat of your hand into it and run your hand up against the pile. If you do the same exercise with an incorrect, soft coat, it will give the impression of being fluffy, silky and soft to the touch, similar to the puppy coat found on Spaniel breeds.

Colour affects the texture and length of outer coat. It is a fact that the dark colours, for example liver or black coats, are shorter in length and are of a more wire texture. The white coat is always longer and softer. Consequently those Wirehairs with a lot of clear, white patches will always be lacking the correct wire texture. However, Wirehairs that are white with liver ticking/roaning will have a better textured coat, because the liver coloured coat, mixing in with the white coat, produces a coarser coat mix. Facial whiskers, to me, put the final touch on the completed picture, but you must not put too much emphasis on these in preference to a correct body coat.

In the show ring we are also seeing more incorrect long, soft coats which have been clippered short. The worrying fact about this is that some judges seem to be totally oblivious to the barbering that has gone on and proceed to place these dogs highly. Consequently newcomers to the breed, seeing such dogs enjoying success, may wish to include these dogs in their breeding programme, with the result that this serious fault is perpetuated.

The signs of a clipped or scissored coat are obvious to an experienced breeder and it would not take a novice too long to spot the same indications. The main clue is that the natural coat on any Wirehair grows to a point. In most animals the growth is never constant and this leaves the hair at varying lengths. A clippered coat leaves the hair tip blunt and squared off and is of a constant length. This consistency occurs when the coat is shaved and then enough time is allowed, before the Wirehair is shown, for the hair to grow sufficiently to cover the clipper marks. The final sign is the deterioration of colour. The more a wire coat is clippered, the more damage there is to the texture. The coat will eventually go soft and woolly and, as the texture changes, so does the colour, going from rich liver to a grey fawn. Those exhibitors who are resorting to these tactics in coat preparation should be aware that the 'woolly coats' we used to get in the late 1970s were often of this grey/fawn colour, so short cuts in coat preparation now are certainly retrograde steps, whereas we should be striving to improve coats at every opportunity.

COLOUR

Unfortunately the American Standard does not allow black and white in its recognised list of colours. This is a great shame and we can be thankful that the British Standard allows this colour to be included.

GAIT/MOVEMENT

All Standards ask for the movement to be smooth and ground-covering with a definite driving hind action. This is essential for a gundog who, without it, would not be able to last

Sh. Ch. Bareve Beverley Hills displaying the true driving movement which is required in a gundog.

David Dalton.

Full Champion Ch. Texson of Tickencote, owned by Peter and Mary Howard. It is essential to breed Wirehairs that are capable of doing a day's work.

David Dalton.

through a day's shooting. I feel that more could be done by Wirehair breeders in this direction by making good, sound movement more of a priority when contemplating the breeding of a litter.

The American Standard asks for the topline to remain firm. Incidentally, those Wirehairs that stand with a roached topline due to the shortness of back nearly always move with the same roaching topline – another reason to maintain the correct proportions and not to encourage those with short backs.

SIZE

Here again the American Standard is more detailed in its description. I totally agree that "correct size and balance are essential" and that dogs either over or under the specified height must be severely penalized. A few years ago we had a problem in that a fair number of males being shown were over the height Standard. I feel we recognised and accepted this and most of the breeders made the effort to redress the situation. A far more serious problem, at the present time, seems to be the number of big, coarse 'doggy' bitches being shown. If this trend continues, we shall have a situation where little, if any, difference exists between the sexes. A male should always appear masculine, preferably with a little stallion-like presence about him, whilst the female should be obviously feminine.

Chapter Six

THE SHOW RING

THE SHOW-GOING TEMPERAMENT

If your main interest is in dog shows and becoming involved in competitions, then it is likely that you will have acquired your Wirehair puppy from a recognised show-winning line, so, whether you are contemplating your first show dog, or your first Wirehair, let us consider what the future may bring. I feel that temperament in a show dog is incredibly important because you may only show your Wirehair for approximately thirty days in any one year, but you will be living together for three hundred and sixty-five days every year. You will therefore understand that your own temperament is also of great importance.

You may think that you are relatively easy-going and will enjoy days out among fellow Wirehair owners, regardless of show placings. However, it is a sad fact but true that some people do not accept defeat gracefully and exhibit dogs either to satisfy their own egos, or to achieve a feeling of self-importance. Too few, in my opinion, actually want to learn more about the breed and enjoy a pleasant hobby. Some will, in a very short time, consider that they have sufficient knowledge of their chosen breed and have become experts. Why is it that some owners, who have only been in their chosen breeds for very few years, feel that they do not need to continue to learn? Knowledge is not something that can be achieved quickly.

The showing of dogs in general is already very popular and increasing annually. Success will come to those owners who are prepared to learn how to show their dogs to the best advantage. If you are a complete novice then you will certainly need advice to train both yourself and your puppy.

SHOW TRAINING

You should enrol at a local training school when your puppy's vaccination programme has been successfully completed. Attending either a ring-craft class or an Obedience class is essential, as they are ideal for teaching both of you how to mix and be sociable with other dogs and owners. Temperament and showmanship are very important with a show dog. Consequently, socialising is a necessity and you must keep your Wirehair accustomed to being with people and being handled by them; then being handled by judges later in life will pose no problems. While you are waiting for the 'all clear' from the vaccination programme you can start teaching basic commands, in the safety of your own home. It is advisable to have covered all of these, and walking on a lead, before you start show training.

One of the first lessons is teaching the command Stand. In the early stages do not try to achieve perfection: just encourage your puppy to stand still on this instruction. As soon as that has been done, give lots of praise and move on to something else. Once it seems that this is being mastered without any movement, then increase the amount of time during which the position must be held.

Another lesson is showing the bite, the teeth. In the early days, a quick parting of the lips is sufficient. Do not prolong this exercise because that will only encourage your puppy to pull away. Obviously, at the start, a mouth inspection by you will be tolerated more readily than one done by a stranger. By the time you attend training classes, this should be something which causes no problems at all. It is very worthwhile because there are some considerate judges who prefer exhibitors to show the dog's bite themselves. This prevents any possibility of spreading infections from dog to dog, which could happen if the judges handled each dog's mouth.

Once you have mastered the basic procedures at home, your puppy will probably be safely over the vaccination programme and ready to socialise. Now is the time to enrol in the training class and learn more about show training. Do not try to do too much too soon. Use the first couple of visits to sit and watch the proceedings and, when you feel that both your puppy and yourself are relaxed, then have a go. Do not be forced into premature participation.

Unfortunately, I find that some trainers in these classes do seem to draw out the procedure of handling unnecessarily. This ends up with your puppy becoming bored and fidgety. I would suggest that a pleasant request to the trainer to be as quick as possible would help until your puppy learns to hold the standing position for a little longer. Once this routine is familiar, then it is quite reasonable to expect your puppy to extend the stand long enough for a judge to complete an examination.

When you come to moving your Wirehair for the trainer, or judge, it is far more satisfying to do this on a loose lead. Therefore, it is worthwhile making the effort to teach your puppy to move this way, rather than by being strung up. The right speed also needs to be mastered. You need to move at a pace that will keep your puppy trotting along beside you, rather than running or pacing, which is a fast, ugly, ambling gait.

The training classes will also teach you and your puppy the basic movements that are used in the show ring. For example, going around the ring in a large circle, in addition to straight lines, both with and without other dogs. There is also the movement called the triangle, where you move away from the judge at an angle, with your dog being held in your left hand. Then you turn left and move parallel with the judge, then turn left again and go back to the judge and the position from which you started. In this movement you need to keep your Wirehair on your left, so that your dog is on the inside and can be seen clearly by the judge at all times. Please do try to remember, whenever you are asked by the judge to move your Wirehair, to position yourself so that your dog can be seen without your legs becoming an obstruction, even if it means changing the side on which your dog normally walks.

By the time your Wirehair puppy has reached six months of age, both of you should feel fairly confident and be proficient in all the basic requirements. Then you need to try and

First lessons in standing. Remember to give lots of praise when your puppy responds correctly.

Am. Ch. Geronimo's Flying Warrior and his daughter, Am. Ch. Weidenhugel Vanessa Warrior, who gained her Championship aged six months and three weeks. Carl Lindemaier.

Sh. Ch. Bareve Bronx, litter brother to breed record holder Beverley Hills. The skill of the handler is to present the dog to full advantage.

David Dalton.

obtain valuable experience. Be guided by the trainers at the training classes and start with some of the local, smaller shows rather than at the top level Championship shows.

AT THE SHOW

Whatever level of show you eventually attend, remember that it is important to ensure that both you and your puppy enjoy the day. Do not arrive late, because, if you do, you will almost certainly have to rush straight into the ring without having a chance to settle or to groom your dog. If this happens it is likely that you will be very tense and this will certainly be transferred straight down the lead to your puppy.

When you do go into the ring try to act calmly. If your puppy is not as well behaved as is normal at training classes, then do not get upset. Everything will be strange for both of you. Just try to make the most of your time in the ring and think about how to present your puppy to the best advantage. Also, bear in mind that you are showing your dog, rather than yourself. Keep your eyes on the judge and, while someone else's dog is being inspected, take the opportunity to check that your Wirehair is still standing properly. You will have time to correct the stance before the judge comes around.

Often puppies will pull and bounce in excitement, instead of moving collectedly across the ring. There is no need to become embarrassed, as this just shows the enjoyment your puppy is experiencing, which is hard to contain. Judges rarely object to puppies playing up in this way. However, you will need to try and control this enthusiasm, so you may have to stop and correct your puppy by giving a sharp command and attempt the movement again. Incidentally, most judges will remain patient, providing that they can see that you have made an improvement in the situation. But do not expect the judge to continue being patient if your puppy disobeys your sharp command and persists in being naughty. Remember that you have paid a sum of money to show your Wirehair under a particular judge, so it is therefore in your own best interests to ensure a good performance. A judge only has a certain amount of time for each dog.

If you are lucky, you may be rewarded by winning a place at the end of the class, but in some classes you may be unplaced. It really should not matter what the end result is, providing that both of you have enjoyed every minute of the experience. Once you have been to several shows, you will soon know if you have enjoyed them sufficiently to continue and progress upwards through the various levels of shows available. If, however, you decide that the dog showing game is not for you, then you can at least say that you gave it a go.

THE JUDGE

No two judges read and interpret Breed Standards in exactly the same way. Different people will have different preferences, whether for soundness of movement or correct breed type or good temperaments. As exhibitors, we should be grateful that judges do not interpret Breed Standards identically, because, if they did, the same dogs would be placed in the same way at every show and there would be little point in running dog shows. Regardless of the end results, dog shows depend on one judge's opinion on that particular day. There is nothing to prevent you asking for the judge's opinion of your dog, but it is advisable to wait until the judging is completed. Remember that if you have asked a judge for an opinion, it may not be entirely complimentary and, if you are not prepared to listen to those views without becoming upset and annoyed, then it is better not to ask. One final point is that, whether you agree or not, the judge's decision is final.

BAD SPORTSMANSHIP

It is a sad fact that the majority of exhibitors attending dog shows are no longer doing it for the fun of competing. Nowadays it seems to be more about winning. People seem to forget that, regardless of what decisions the judge makes, they are still taking home the same wonderful dog they arrived with. Your Wirehair never gets upset about losing, so why should you? If you feel that you do not enjoy being beaten by other Wirehairs and their owners, then you really should consider not continuing showing.

New exhibitors can get disgruntled if the same Wirehairs and the same owners win consistently. They should try to understand that if the same one keeps on winning, it may well be because it is the best Wirehair there on the day. Likewise, when the same owners keep on winning, perhaps it is because their Wirehairs, coming from an established line, are of a similar type. If this happens to be the type that a particular judge prefers, then an eventual unbeaten line-up will reflect this.

Remember, when showing, that if you do not have a successful day, there will always be another day to look forward to. Along with the competitive spirit, we must keep a sense of proportion and remember that we are gathered together, or we should be, for the betterment and progress of the German Wirehaired Pointer.

Chapter Seven

THE WIREHAIR IN BRITAIN

This chapter has been compiled with the co-operation of the Wirehair owners in the United Kingdom at the present time in order to give a comprehensive picture of the breed in this country and the people who care about it. It is interesting to remember that the Kennel Club only granted 'Championship Status' to the breed as recently as 1986 and we already have ten full Champions, that is, Wirehairs who have won the title of Show Champion and have also won a Field Trial award. This is a tremendous feat when you consider that the more popular gundog breeds rarely produce full Champions. All dogs, in the following pages, are introduced by their breed title but subsequent references use the family name by which the dog is known.

ANDESHEIM: MAJOR GEORGE WILKINSON

Major George Wilkinson first met the Wirehairs while he was stationed in Germany at the end of the Second World War. He was a great sporting and shooting man who trained dogs both for his own use and for other people. He did not buy a Wirehair then because, for several years, his career took him around the world and he found that both Cocker and Springer Spaniels were easier to obtain. On leaving the Army he bought a German Shorthaired Pointer. In 1972 a friend of his, Bill Warner, was contemplating importing a Wirehair from Germany because he wanted a really good pointing, rough shooting dog. He had no thoughts about the show ring. However, Major Wilkinson had the idea that he would like to purchase a puppy from this import. The two of them went to Germany and selected Vrede von Romersee. She was therefore the first Wirehair to be imported into this country since those few brought in by the demobbed soldiers in the early fifties.

When Bill considered that it was time to breed from Vrede he had two options. Either he could use a dog called Chang, who was a typical Wirehair and an excellent worker but unfortunately had Shorthair blood in his immediate ancestry, or he could import again. He chose the second option and brought in two litter brother-and-sister black and white Wirehairs. They were Vassel v.d. Bocholter and Vicky v.d. Bocholter, who went to Major Wilkinson.

Vicky v.d. Bocholter was the first Wirehair to be shown in this Country and came second in the Any Variety Not Separately Classified at Windsor and was also the first Wirehair to be officially invited to parade at the annual Game Fair.

An Andesheim youngster related to the Bocholter imports.

On February 12th 1976, Vicky whelped a litter sired by the Dutch imported dog, Rakker van de Mijzijde. From that litter came Major Wilkinson's Andesheim Alfons v d Heide who was named after Alfons Wischerhoff, the shooting friend who had helped in the selection of Vrede von Romersee. This was the first Wirehair to gain a Kennel Club Stud Book number by virtuc of his wins in Field Trials. He was also the first Wirehair winner of a Field Trial. That was on October 1st 1977 in the Hungarian Vizsla Club Novice Stake. On October 8th 1977 he gained a Certificate of Merit at the German Shorthaired Pointcr Club Novice Stake. Alfons had also won several show awards in Any Variety classes long before separate Wirehair breed classes were introduced.

Alfons seemed to be set for a fine Field Trial career but was unfortunately killed in a road accident before his third birthday. It was about this time that Wittekind Bennie von Andesheim (who was originally owned by my mother and myself) was returned to his breeder, Mieneke Mills de Hoog, because he would not allow judges to handle him in the show ring. In view of Alfons' tragic accident, Mieneke gave Bennie to Major Wilkinson.

Bennie, who was then two years of age, had not had any working training until he joined Major Wilkinson. His natural ability was such that he soon adapted to his new life-style and had won the Hungarian Vizsla Club's Novice Stake within his first year of Trialling. Due to Major Wilkinson's advancing years, Bennie was not Field Trialled extensively, but he did become Major Wilkinson's rough shooting companion and also became the first official Wirehair Deer-tracker. It was in this sphere that he excelled and he became proficient in the Bringsel method. Major Wilkinson and Bennie gave many demonstrations to the British Deer Society courses run by Dieter Dent at Stockbridge.

During 1979 Major Wilkinson imported a German bitch called Sissi vom Reiler Hals-

Andesheim who was in whelp to Baron von Reiler Hals. Both these two Wirehairs were noted Field Trial award winners in their native Germany. Sissi whelped in quarantine but unfortunately only four puppies survived. Andesheim Ziggi and Zoe went to Mr and Mrs Leonard Durman Walters, Andesheim Zia went to Mr John Birth, and Andesheim Zita went to Mr Barron from Northern Ireland.

Major Wilkinson has been an active member of the German Wirehaired Pointer Club since the outset, has held the position of Chairman and has been President since 1983.

BAREVE: BARBARA AND SHARON PINKERTON

I own the Bareve prefix in partnership with my mother, Barbara Pinkerton, and we have been active in dogs for a number of years. Barbara's first dog was a Chastleton Springer which she had when she was was nine years of age and she bred her first litter (jointly registered with her father, the late Mr Marshall – affix O'Frankley) before she left school. The prefix of Bareve originates from being part of her name joined with the name of her first dog, a Boxer, Eve.

I was introduced to the show scene by winning second place with my own Cocker Spaniel, Chadleigh Golden Sunset, at the Brent Show in 1968. Even though the family had lived with Boxers, Great Danes, Greyhounds and Cocker Spaniels, when I was was nine years old I saw a picture of the Wirehair in a library book and I vowed that one day I would have one. The book did say that the Wirehair was not readily available in the United Kingdom at that time, so I continued to show the Greyhounds and Cocker Spaniels at both Open and Championship shows until Mieneke Mills de Hoog imported her Dutch Wirehair. Then we made contact with Mieneke and waited until she felt that she had a Wirehair that could be shown.

On October 16th 1977 we collected Wittekind Bennie after he had competed in Wirehair Classes held at the German Shorthaired Pointer Club Show. Bennie was ten months of age and was a very strong character who soon wormed his way into our hearts. He was a super companion who detested being kept in a run. He continually climbed out, and was at his happiest roaming free around the stables. Unfortunately he did not like the show ring and, on occasions, flatly refused to be handled by judges. On the occasions when he did co-operate, he was successful, winning Best Wirehair male at the Hammersmith Gold Medal Show in 1978 and, later that year, he was Reserve Best Any Variety Not Separately Classified Dog to an Otterhound who subsequently went on to win Reserve in the Hound Group at Crufts.

I decided that I wanted to continue to show Wirehairs and, as Bennie detested the shows so much, he was returned to Mieneke, who suggested he would be more suited to the working home of Major Wilkinson. Then, on October 22nd 1978, we collected Bennie's first registered daughter who was just turned five weeks. Collecting Eva at such an early age was Mieneke's idea, so that we would have a better chance of getting the temperament right and therefore of having a Wirehair to show. As it turned out, Eva was a bubbling, extrovert character who completely took over the Bareve household.

She became Sh. Ch. Wittekind Eva Braun at Bareve and was the breed's most prolific show winner of that era. At six months and two days she won Best Wirehair puppy and Best

Sh. Ch. Wittekind Eva Braun at Bareve, the first Show Champion bitch, owned by the Bareve kennel.

Sandy Plunkett.

Bareve Baldur creating breed history at SKC in 1983 when winning the Gundog Group.

David Lindsay.

of Breed at the Hammersmith Gold Medal Show. There were few opportunities in separate breed classes in the early eighties, so that most of her winning was done in Any Variety Not Separately Classified and Rare Breed Classes against different breeds. Her first Best Bitch in Breed award at a Championship was the National Gundog Show in 1980, under Michael Boothroyd. Quite remarkably, she has been the Best Bitch in Breed at every National Gundog August show since 1980, up to the time of winning the BCC and Best of Breed in 1986, under her breeder, Mieneke.

Eva won well at Cruft's, including Best AVNSC in 1984, was shortlisted in the final six of the Gundog Group under Mary Roslin-Williams, and won the breed's first-ever Bitch Challenge Certificate under Mrs B. Farrand in 1986. She was the top winning Wirehair bitch for 1981 and the top winning Wirehair overall for 1982, 1983 and 1984. In 1983 she was Best in Show at the German Wirehaired Pointer Club's first Club Show, held at Peterborough under Jean Lanning. She also gained the honour of being the first-ever Wirehair to become Show Champion bitch, which she did at the Welsh Kennel Club in August 1986, just weeks short of her eighth birthday.

Eva's litter born in February 1981 was to Mieneke's Swedish import, Mr Allround of Wittekind. Bareve Baldur, Brunhilde and Bianca were retained by Barbara and Sharon, and Sh. Ch. Bareve Bonne of Fleetapple went to George and Di Arrowsmith. Baldur and Brunhilde were shown extensively and were successful in both breed and variety classes.

Breed History was made in May 1983 when Joan Wells Meacham gave Baldur the Gundog Group at the Scottish Kennel Club Championship show, the first-ever group winner for the breed.

Brunhilde and Bianca went on to produce superb quality puppies with similar trustworthy temperaments. Brunhilde produced a litter to Ch. Wittekind Helmut, who was the breed's first full Champion, and Sh. Ch. Bareve Barmelton and Bareve Baringa were retained. Bianca's first litter was sired by Wittekind Ice King and produced Bareve Brombeere, who became the breed's first Junior Warrant winner.

Baringa was not extensively shown because preference was given to Barmelton. However she still managed to win Best AVNSC at Cruft's in 1986, under Mr S. Wilberg, at the tender age of one year and six days old. Barmelton's success was considerable, being the top winning Wirehair bitch and joint overall in 1985 and gaining her title in 1987. Barmelton's showing highlight came in 1988 when she won the Gundog Group at Driffield Championship show and became only the breed's second such winner.

During 1982 it became apparent that new blood was desperately needed and we decided that we would consider importing a Wirehair male. Bearing in mind the breed's country of origin, we went on the Wirehair Club's trip to Germany to see if we could import a male that would suit the Bareve line. Unfortunately, although the Wirehairs shown were all excellent workers, neither of us were impressed with the displays of sharp temperament shown when the Wirehairs were gathered in close groups. As our own Wirehairs lived peacefully together at home, we decided that we did not want to risk introducing the sharper temperament to our existing stock.

So, having already established close contact with breeders in the United States of America and found that the American dogs had impeccable temperaments combined with working

Am. Ch. Geronimos Knickers Von S.G. at Bareve: The first Champion to be shown in the UK.

Dave Freeman.

Sh. Ch. Bareve Beverley Hills: The breed recordholder.

David Bull.

ability and ring presence, we bought a four-month-old male puppy from Jo Ann Burns. He remained with his breeder until he gained his American Championship and had also been taught the basic gundog work.

Am. Ch. Geronimos Knickers von S.G. at Bareve was, therefore, the first Wirehair Champion to be shown in the United Kingdom. He won extensively in both breed and variety classes and his first major breed win was Best of Breed at the Gundog Breeds Association of Scotland Championship Show in 1984, under breed specialist Andy Daly.

Nevertheless, it was Nikki's progeny which really proved that the importation was an immense success. Bred to Bianca, he produced Sh. Ch. Bareve Beverley Hills, Sh. Ch. Bareve Bronx and Bareve Baltimore at Benreeda, who was owned by Les and Pat Dempster. To Brunhilde he produced Ch. Bareve Frau Holle, owned by Peter and Kath Lomasney.

Sh. Ch. Bareve Beverley Hills is the breed's record holder and has won, to date, twenty-two CCs, four RCCs, Championship show Group Winner at Welks 1991 and Reserve Group Winner at Windsor 1993. Dolly has also won Best of Breed at Crufts for four consecutive years and has been shortlisted in the last six of the Cruft's Gundog Group twice. She was Best in Show at the German Wirehaired Pointers Club's first Championship Show in 1988 under Lyn Briggs, and again under Peggy Grayson in 1992, and also collected the BCC at both the 1990 and the 1991 shows. Dolly was the top winning Wirehair overall in 1988, 1990 and 1991, and top winning bitch for 1993.

Ch. Bareve Frau Holle has won twelve CCs and three RCCs, and has won three Reserve Gundog Groups at Championship Shows – Bath 1989, East of England, and Driffield 1990. Heather had already won a Certificate of Merit at the German Shorthaired Pointer Club Novice stake before winning her third Challenge Certificate, under Pat Chapman, making her the breed's first full Champion bitch.

Nikki's grandchildren are proving to be of excellent temperament and type, which is enabling them to be successful in whatever sphere is selected for them. Bareve Bonneville produced an excellent litter to Mieneke's Wittekind Tracker, before the Wittekinds emigrated to France. The star of the litter is Rudi and Loes Hulsman's Sh. Ch. Bareve Bertold Brecht, who was originally bought as a good, typical companion with an excellent temperament. Known as Jasper, his spectacular introduction to the show scene resulted in him winning the CC and Best in Show at the GWPC Championship Show in his first-ever appearance at the age of fourteen months. He gained his show title in just four shows at sixteen months old. He has gone on to win twelve CCs and five RCCs, he is now the breed's male record holder and he is still only three years of age. He has also won the Gundog Group at Richmond and Reserve Gundog Group at Bath in 1993, was Best in Show at the GWPC Championship shows 1991 and 1993, and was Best of Breed and in the final six of the Gundog Group at Crufts 1993. We retained his sister, Bareve Belotti, Reserve Group winner, and his other sisters – Blitzlicht owned by Alan and Maggie White, and Bosanova owned by Rachel Thompson – have all won CCs and RCCs, accumulating a total of sixteen CCs and twelve RCCs by the four litter mates.

Barmelton produced just one litter, and that was by Bareve Bushranger, who is a full younger brother to Dolly. Sh. Ch. Bareve Bacall, owned by Claire Shaw, has gained two CCs, one at the GWPC Championship show in 1993 and four RCCs.

Sh. Ch. Bareve Bertold Brecht: The male breed recordholder, who I handled to win the Gundog Group at Richmond in 1993. He is owned by Rudi and Loes Hulsman.

John Hartley.

Bareve Bodwane produced a litter by Sh. Ch. Bareve Baton Rouge, and we retained Ch. Bareve Bramble. Bemyca, one CC and seven RCCs, went to Claire Shaw, and Brocade, one CC and one Reserve Challenge Certificate, to Peter and Kath Lomasney. Ch. Bareve Bramble won her show title at two and a half years old and, because of her natural ability, the decision was taken to attempt to get her full qualifier. As I work full-time, the opportunities to teach Folly the basics were somewhat curtailed. In October 1992, due to the sudden death of Peter and Kath's young Wirehair male, Folly was sent over to the Lomansey home in an attempt to help them to get over their upset. Peter was able to devote his time to teaching Folly all that was required of her to win her Show Working Qualifier at the GWPC All-Aged stake at Upton within fourteen weeks of commencing training. Folly has since gone on to win seven CCs and three RCCs, including the BCC at Cruft's in 1992 and 1993. She was also Best of Breed at Cruft's 1992.

I have always had a Wirehair to go shooting with, and I have been constantly badgered, by fellow Field Trial enthusiasts, to enter a Field Trial. Finally, in October 1993, Folly and I entered the Weimaraner Association Novice Stake and won a Certificate of Merit at our first attempt together. This award was most satisfying, as it was confirmation of Folly's full Champion status rather than just winning the more easily achieved Show Working Qualifier.

The Bareve Wirehairs are, without doubt, the top show-winning kennel to date and we have owned or produced ten Show Champions, of which two are full Champions. The Bareve Wirehairs have won a total of eighty-seven CCs and sixty-five RCCs in addition to four home-bred Championship show Gundog Groups and six home-bred Reserve Championship show Gundog Groups. Bareve is still the only kennel that has bred Championship show Group winning Wirehairs.

BENREEDA: LES AND PAT DEMPSTER

After following the Wirehairs for a number of years with the intention of eventually having one, Les and Pat Dempster say that they were lucky to get Bareve Baltimore at Benreeda. Fergus was sired by Am. Ch. Geronimos Knickers von S.G. at Bareve out of Bareve Bianca. At his first outing, which was the National Gundog Championship Show of 1986, he won the RCC, under breed specialist Mieneke Mills de Hoog. His success continued and he won another three RCCs before he had to be retired from the show ring because of an illness which resulted in him not carrying enough condition.

Anka of Roland Rat at Benreeda was bred by Mr Larner, sired by Macdevil Van de

Benreeda Wolfgang of Jacinto CD EX, UD EX, WD EX and TD EX, owned by Terry Hadley.

Bemmeraue-Wittekind out of Pepper Spa. Anka was originally sold to a gamekeeper called Mr Roland Van Oyen, who used to work her. Anka produced a litter, sired by Fergus, and Les and Pat obtained a dog puppy who was named Going Haywire at Benreeda and a bitch called Real Livewire at Benreeda. Shortly after this litter, Mr Van Oyen gave Anka to Les and Pat, who showed her on occasions, resulting in her gaining her stud book number. Unfortunately, the bitch puppy was only shown a few times before she injured her shoulder, which affected her movement, and she was found a suitable home as a pet.

Going Haywire at Benreeda was the top puppy in breed in 1989: he won his Junior Warrant at twelve months and won the CC and Best of Breed at Leicester whilst only twenty months of age. However, tragedy struck: he was found to have a malformed colon and died before he was three years of age.

Fortunately Les and Pat had repeated the mating in November 1990 and retained two dogs, namely Benreeda Walther and Benreeda Wagner. Shortly after they had made their show debuts, Les and Pat had a dog returned to them because his owners' circumstances had changed. Consequently Benreeda Witzig rejoined his brothers and all three dogs have been successful, consistently winning RCCs.

Another dog from the second Benreeda litter is Benreeda Wolfgang of Jacinto, who is owned by Terry Hadley, a top trainer and handler in Working Trials. Terry is delighted that Hogan has already achieved his CD EX, UD EX, WD EX and TD EX qualifications and, at his second attempt in a Ticket Trial, only thirteen months from his first-ever Trial, won the Working Trials CC. Terry states that Hogan is a complete workaholic with a strongly developed natural hunting instinct, boundless energy, quickness in learning, and a wilful but totally loyal, loveable nature. It is no wonder that Terry says Hogan is not the easiest dog to live with and Terry definitely needs eyes in the back of his head!

BRYANTSCROFT: RORY MAJOR

Rory Major has had Labradors and Springer Spaniels since 1977, and one of his first experiences of Wirehairs came when he met Derek Beavan's Juams Bee Bee of Hillbury. Then, on a visit to Major Wilkinson's kennels to check the progress of his boss's two Shorthairs who had been sent to Major Wilkinson for training, he saw a litter of Wirehair puppies. These puppies were by Major Wilkinson's Wittekind Bennie von Andesheim out of a bitch called Andesheim Asta v.d. Heide, who was owned by Mr G. Chiari but was kept with Major Wilkinson.

Major Wilkinson persuaded Rory that he should have a Wirehair addition to his gundog team. Having been assured that he was doing the correct thing, Rory chose the hairiest bitch puppy, who kept pushing her head through the fence. This twelve-week-old black and white puppy was called Velia von Andesheim and was to be the breed's first and, to date, only Field Trial Champion. Velia was very slow to develop and extremely unsure of herself. Rory decided to train her along the already tested method he uses when training his Labradors. This proved to be successful, even though she was still very sensitive and, if she felt she was being pushed to achieve something, would instantly pack up and refuse to do any more.

In May 1985 she produced a solitary black and white bitch puppy, sired by Stablaheim Clansman, named Bryantscroft Solo. Rory retained her until she was six months of age and

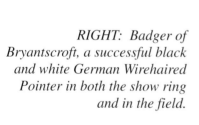

ABOVE: Field Trial Champion Velia von Andesheim: The only Field Trial Champion to date, pictured with a season's trophies. Owned by Rory Major.

RIGHT: Badger of Bryantscroft, a successful black and white German Wirehaired Pointer in both the show ring and in the field.

it was then that Lyn and Mike Bower fell for her and asked to have her. Rory agreed but stated that, when she was eventually bred from, he would like to have a puppy back. After Velia's litter she returned to work and was found to be stronger and considerably better at her work than she was before her maternal duties. It was just six months later, on November 16th 1985, that she won her second Open Stake at the Weimaraner Club of Great Britain and gained her Field Trial Champion title. Velia's Field Trial career is outstanding, winning a total of twenty-five Field Trial awards, including sixteen first prizes, of which six are first in Open Trials, five second prizes and an incredible third place in the Hunting, Pointing,

Retrieving Field Trial Championship. In June 1988 Bryantscroft Solo was put to Cannylad Congressman and a litter was produced. This time Rory chose a black and white dog puppy as he felt that a male would be harder going in the field. This puppy became Badger of Bryantscroft, who has had success in both the field and the show ring, gaining his Junior Warrant. To date Badger has won eight Field Trial awards and has qualified to run in the HPR Field Trial Championship. It is very interesting to note that, up to now, Velia and Badger are the only Wirehairs that have qualified to run in the HPR Field Trial Championship.

Rory feels that not only do Wirehairs make excellent working dogs, but they are also good house dogs and companions, having readily accepted Rory's and Jane's young daughters. However, as a working dog, Rory feels that the Wirehair has not really progressed at all from the original dogs that were bred from the early imports of both Major Wilkinson and Mieneke Mills de Hoog, and are not the force they should be in Field Trials.

FLEETAPPLE: GEORGE AND DI ARROWSMITH

In 1981 George and Di Arrowsmith bought Bareve Bonne of Fleetapple, who was sired by Mr Allround of Wittekind out of Sh. Ch. Wittekind Eva Braun at Bareve. She became a great ambassador for the breed, possessing a super nature and adoring all humans and animals she met. As with most Wirehairs being shown in that era, most of her winning was done in AVNSC and AV Rare Breeds, well before breed classes became established. She also gained numerous Best of Breeds and Best Opposite Sex at Championship level before the Wirehairs were granted Championship status.

In April 1985 Rosie produced a litter of puppies sired by Desert Mills Henry Tickencote, most of which were sold to shooting homes and all of which are good companions. Rosie gained her Show Championship, winning her first CC at Birmingham National under Helen Case Shelley, her second under Ferelith Hamilton at the Scottish Kennel Club and her third

Sh. Ch. Bareve Bonne of Fleetapple on point, owned by George and Di Arrowsmith. Anne Johnson.

at Richmond under Dick Finch with her mother Eva Braun winning the RCC.

Rosie was really George's shooting dog but he allowed Di to 'borrow' her to show. Once she had gained her title, he claimed her back and she continued to be his honest and loyal shooting companion until 1991. Then she made an unusual appearance in the Veteran class at Cruft's 1991, but sustained a nasty fall during the day. Whilst she appeared to be unhurt at the time, she later developed a severe back problem and had, subsequently, to be retired from the field.

KATH AND PETER LOMASNEY

Peter first became interested in Wirehairs when he acquired a Goshawk and needed a dog to accompany him. Having looked at the several breeds that were available to choose from, he decided on the Wirehair because of the breed's weatherproof coat and well-known working ability. One other important factor was the need for a good temperament, because the Wirehair was destined to be a family companion as well as being Peter's working dog.

In 1984 Kath and Peter made contact with Sally Williams, who had a litter by Bareve Baldur out of her bitch St. Germains Buffy, and they returned home with Matilde Renata. Known as Bracken, her temperament was everything that both Kath and Peter wanted, as she was totally trustworthy with their children, Matthew and Sarah. At that stage, Matthew was having to spend a considerable amount of time on crutches but, even through Bracken was still quite young and excitable, she would instantly be steadier with Matthew.

As for Bracken's training, it was entirely down to trial and error and a little help from any books that could be found. No gundog trainer wanted to help Peter with this rare breed and they repeatedly told him that he should have bought a Labrador. So Peter and Bracken determinedly continued helping each other, and she eventually became the working companion both Peter and his Goshawk wanted.

Having been GWPC members since obtaining Bracken, the Lomasneys had been

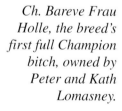

Ch. Bareve Frau Holle, the breed's first full Champion bitch, owned by Peter and Kath Lomasney.

John Hartley.

introduced to the show scene and decided that they should support what few breed classes were around. Nevertheless they realised that, although Bracken was everything they wanted, she would never be an ideal show dog. So, in late 1985 Kath and Peter, having already made contact with my mother and myself because we owned Bracken's father, booked a bitch puppy that they could show and work.

They waited until Bareve Brunhilde whelped her litter in February 1986 to Am. Ch. Geronimos Knickers von S.G. at Bareve, and, soon after, Bareve Frau Holle joined the Lomasney home. Heather soon became established as a real family dog joining in all the activities, with Peter teaching her the working side, Kath showing her, and becoming, first and foremost, a companion to them all.

Her early career was impressive considering that she was only sparingly shown. Her first Challenge Certificate and Best of Breed was won at Leeds 1987 whilst still only a Junior, and her second CC, also with Best of Breed, was won at National Gundog just weeks later. Each time Heather was short-listed in the Gundog Group. The highlight of 1987 was when Heather was Best in Show at the GWPC Open Show under breed specialist Pat Chapman. Heather's training continued and, on the 26th January 1988, she was entered in the German Shorthaired Pointer Club's Novice stake at Brocket Park. She and Peter had a successful day which ended with them being awarded a Certificate of Merit, in addition to the guns award.

At Leicester Championship show in August 1988, history was made when Pat Chapman gave Heather her third CC and Best of Breed, making her the first full Champion Wirehair bitch in the United Kingdom. Heather's show career then took off and she finished 1989 by being the top winning Wirehair bitch, in addition to winning the Reserve Gundog Group at Bath Championship show. In 1990 Heather added to her Championship show Group Reserve by winning another two such awards, at East of England Championship show and Driffield Championship show.

In April 1991 Heather took time out to have a litter by Sh. Ch. Bareve Baton Rouge and a dog puppy was retained. He was Bareve Beinn Eighe, known as Rowan, who made an impressive start to his show career, gaining his Junior Warrant, one CC and two RCCs. Unfortunately, tragedy struck with his sudden death in October 1992.

Bareve Brocade, known as Fearn, joined Kath and Peter in 1989 and, although she has been successful in the show ring, winning one CC and one RCC, it is as a working dog that she excels. She is a fearless, outgoing hunting dog who spends most of her time accompanying Peter and the Goshawk to Falconry meetings. So exceptional is she that she has been worked successfully by other Falconry members with their birds and has, on more than one occasion, been given the Best Gundog award of the meeting. Bareve Boomerang joined Kath and Peter in 1993. Fraser is sired by Sh. Ch. Bareve Baton Rouge out of Bareve Bodwane and is a full brother to Fearn. Whilst obviously just commencing his show career, he is the top winning puppy in breed for 1993, despite being sparingly shown.

CLAIRE SHAW

Claire's introduction to the breed was gradual. She was fascinated by Pat Chapman's bitch, Lorelei of Wittekind at Shargleam, known as Hannah, and spent most show days sitting with her while Pat was busy with her Flatcoats. When Hannah had her litter by Bareve Baldur in

May 1983, Claire chose a male puppy, who became Shargleam Rudesheim.

Rudi was a charming puppy with an easy-going, bomb-proof nature. Claire and Rudi attended obedience and gundog classes in an effort to curtail his determined character. They became dedicated supporters of the breed. Claire showed him and Pat's Hannah at every opportunity that arose, in AVNSC, Rare Breeds and breed classes. At all times, during Rudi's show career, he was renowned for his excellent temperament and character of a level rarely seen in Wirehair males. Rudi campaigned regularly and was a consistent winner at all levels, winning two RCCs.

In September 1989, Claire purchased a bitch puppy from my Bareve kennel, called Bareve Bemyca. Flame is sired by Sh. Ch. Bareve Baton Rouge out of Bareve Bodwane and is a perfect angel. Compared to Rudi, Claire finds Flame really easy to live with. As with Rudi, Flame has been regularly shown at all levels and has been extremely successful. To date she has won one CC and Best of Breed and seven RCCs.

In November 1990, after waiting for some time, Claire finally got a bitch puppy from her long-time favourite bitch, Sh. Ch. Bareve Barmelton, sired by Bareve Bushranger. Sh. Ch. Bareve Bacall, known as Moth, has so much energy, such an abundance of enthusiasm – and is extremely sociable. She is always a delight to meet at shows, because she is always happy, throws back her head and "woo woo wooos" at everyone.

Moth has been a consistent winner in the show ring and, to date, has won three CCs and four RCCs. The highlight of her show career so far was winning her title at Crufts 1994, along with Best of Breed.

SUNHOUSE: RUTH AND DOUG MARTIN

The Sunhouse kennel of German Wirehaired Pointers was established in 1979 when Ruth and Doug Martin purchased Wiggmansburg Leonardo of Sunhouse as an eleven week old puppy from Leonard and Diana Durman-Walters. Fritz was sired by Wittekind Achtung out of Wittekind Blanche. Fritz, at the age of seven years old, won the first DCC available at Crufts 1986 under Mrs B. Farrand, gained his title at the National Gundog Show under Mieneke Mills de Hoog, and became the first Wirehair Show Champion.

Sh. Ch. Wiggmansburg Leonardo of Sunhouse, the first Show Champion, owned by Doug and Ruth Martin.

In 1980 Ruth and Doug purchased another puppy from Leonard and Diana, but this time it was a bitch puppy, Wiggmansburg Mystique Of Sunhouse, by Andesheim Ziggi von Wiggmansburg out of Wiggmansburg Blanche. Eventually, in March 1986, she produced a litter sired by Wittekind Tallisman of Lufbra, which was to be the first Sunhouse litter. From this litter came Sh. Ch. Sunhouse Alfonz de Wolfe, who gained his title at LKA in December 1991, and Ch. Sunhouse Elena Mistalai of Normbar who won a Certificate of Merit in addition to her two CCs by 1990 but, unfortunately, had to wait until Richmond 1992 to gain her third CC. During 1985 Wirewood Dynamic of Sunhouse was purchased and was campaigned to her Show Champion title in 1990. In 1988 Tallisman was bought and he, too, gained his Show Champion title in 1989. Additionally, in 1989, Ruth and Doug repeated the mating of Tallisman to Mystique, which produced a further two title holders.

TICKENCOTE: PETER AND MARY HOWARD

Peter and Mary Howard's first Wirehair was Wittekind Fraulein, who was bred by Mieneke Mills de Hoog in July 1979 and sired by Wittekind Achtung out of Heliose. Peter's main interest at that time was the working ability of the Wirehair and he preferred to concentrate on that rather than the Show ring. However, Mary did show Meg and had considerable success, including Best AVNSC bitch at Cruft's in 1982.

Meg proved her working ability by winning numerous Field Trial awards, including first in an All Aged Stake at Bicester, third in an Open Stake in Somerley and a third in a Champion Stake in Ardlee, Ireland. Both Peter and Meg had also been invited to give working demonstrations at the Game Fair.

In September 1982 Desert Mills Henry Tickencote arrived in quarantine, aged fifteen weeks. He had been imported from Helen Case Shelley and was the first American import to arrive in the UK. His temperament was guaranteed and the only danger Mary had when she first visited him was of being licked to death. As he arrived while he was still so young, his working and show training could not be started until his six months quarantine had finished. However, as soon as he was released, Tex began his training and the long process of getting him fit commenced.

His first award was second place in a Novice Field Trial whilst he was under two years of age. He has since gone on to win ten Field Trial awards in addition to his one CC, gained under his breeder Helen Case Shelley at the Birmingham National, and two RCCs.

Ch. Texson of Tickencote was bred by John and Sharon Blackmore in April 1984 and was sired by Tex out of their bitch Wittekind Ingeborg. He gained his third CC at Richmond in 1988 but, as he had already won Field Trial awards, he became the breed's third full Champion. He eventually achieved five CCs and five RCCs in addition to winning Best in Show at the GWPC show in 1985 and six Field Trial placements.

Ch. Jayah of Tickencote was born in May 1985 and was bred by Greta Ricketts. He, too, was sired by Tex and was out of Meg's litter sister, Wittekind Frederika. Jayah was extremely successful in the show ring, winning his title at the Welsh Kennel Club show in 1989 and ending up being the top overall Wirehair in 1989. He was the first Wirehair male to win his Junior Warrant and won a total of ten CCs, six RCCs and Best in Show at the GWPC Championship show in 1991.

Ch. Wittekind Helmut, the breed's first full Champion, owned by Ron and Hilde Hilson.

David Dalton.

WITTEKIND: MIENEKE MILLS DE HOOG

Mieneke Mills de Hoog's Wittekind kennels were responsible for the foundation stock of most of today's show and working lines in the United Kingdom. Having been associated with German Shorthaired Pointers for a number of years, Mieneke introduced the Wirehairs to her already successful kennel in 1975, with the Dutch imports. She originally selected an unrelated male and female for Tony Vaughan and an additional unrelated female for herself. However, all three were imported in Mieneke's name and were subsequently transferred into Tony Vaughan's ownership. In March 1976 Tony bred a litter from his two Dutch imports, Rakker van de Mijzijde and Heliose. Shortly afterwards, due to pressure of work, Tony transferred his imports into Mieneke's name.

The first Wittekind litter was born on the 21st August 1976 and, as Mieneke's Wirehair litters followed the alphabet, they were all registered with names beginning with the letter 'A'. The A litter was sired by Rakker out of Mieneke's Dutch import Matilde Vant Staringsland to Wittekind. The second Wittekind litter was born on the 11th December 1976 and was sired by Rakker out of Heliose. Wittekind Blanche formed the foundation of the Wiggmansburg line, Wittekind Bennie formed the Bareve line, Wittekind Bernadette went to John Lamb, Wittekind Brunhilde formed the Albany line, and Wittekind Briggs joined Lyn and John Briggs, who had already obtained Lanka Blitz vom Insul and Lanka Bertha von Insul. At Cruft's in 1977 Matilde was Best AVNSC and was shown on the subsequent Cruft's television programme.

The C litter followed, almost a year later in November 1977, and was sired by Wittekind Brown Foxie out of Matilde. Wittekind Cleo, after being successfully shown in the United Kingdom, was exported to Australia and Wittekind Count Barinsky was eventually exported

Mr Allround of Wittekind with his son, Wittekind Jack Frost, with Mieneke and Laura Mills
de Hoog.   *David Henley.*

to Sweden. Mieneke repeated the already successful B litter in May 1978 and, in September, followed with the fifth Wittekind litter. The E litter produced Wittekind Eva Braun at Bareve, who joined the Bareve's. The F litter followed in July 1979, and that was sired by Wittekind Achtung out of Heliose. The G litter was a half brother and sister mating between Wittekind Brigadoon out of Wittekind Aufweidershen. The next litter was the H litter, born in March 1980, and that produced Wittekind Helmut, who joined Wittekind Fredrich with Ron and Hilda Hilson, and Wittekind Hans who was exported to Mrs M. Beeney in America.

In September 1980 Mr Allround of Wittekind was released from quarantine. He was known as Oscar, was hip dysplasia free, and was imported from Sweden by Mieneke to improve the Wirehair's temperament and coat and to add substance and bone. This was the new blood that was desperately needed to mix with the existing lines. The next six Wittekind litters were by Mr Allround, who had already made an impact in the show ring. For fellow show exhibitors it was a welcome change to be able to walk down the benches, see Oscar beckoning to people to touch him, and know this could be done in complete safety. At Cruft's 1981 Oscar topped the AVNSC section, under Harry Glover, and appeared later in the Gundog Group. Tragically Oscar died in early January 1982, and the subsequent post mortem report revealed nothing.

However, Oscar had stamped his type on his progeny, who were noted for their good temperaments. There were numerous winning Oscar offspring in both the show ring and the field. They included Wittekind Ingeborg, owned by John and Sharon Blackmore, Wittekind Jack Frost, owned by David and Chris Henley, who was successful in both spheres, Wittekind Jutta at Bareve owned by our Bareve kennel, and Lorelei of Wittekind at Shargleam, owned by Pat Chapman.

For two years Mieneke searched the world for a Wirehair stud dog to bring in as a replacement for Oscar. She did fall for the German-bred Dutch Field Trial Champion, Quell von der Wupperaue, who had won the Hegewald Auslage Prufung Bestanden at only nineteen months of age. Unfortunately Quell, by then seven years old, was not for sale. Mieneke eventually managed to buy an in-bred three-month-old male puppy (father ex daughter) called Macdevil Van de Bemmeraue-Wittekind who, unfortunately, developed parvovirus in quarantine, which set him back somewhat.

Devil's first litter was to Matilde and produced the T litter born in June 1984, with Wittekind Tallisman of Lufbra going to Ann Moorhouse and Ann Dawson. One of his next litters was to Leona of Wittekind, in September 1984, and this produced Wittekind Dare Devil who became Mieneke's first Wittekind-owned Show Champion and later qualified as a full Champion. Unfortunately for the British Wirehair owners, Mieneke and all the Wittekind dogs, apart from three old Wirehair bitches who were left with Liesbeth Mills, went to live in France in September 1990.

Chapter Eight

THE WIREHAIR IN NORTH AMERICA

The Wirehair is more popular in America than it is in the UK or Canada. In this chapter, I review some of the leading kennels and the influential Wirehairs based in the US and in Canada. The kennels and dogs are featured in alphabetical order, for convenience.

AFTERHOURS: WALT AND TINA WHITMORE
This kennel is the home of the current top, living, American sire, whose progeny includes thirty-two Champions. He is very close to becoming the top registered German Wirehaired Pointer sire to date. He is Am. Ch. Shurcan Baron of AfterHours, who went to Walt and Tina Whitmore at ten weeks old. He was bred by James and Barbara Halligan and Patricia Laurans and sired by Amigo Vom Hedge Row, who was all-German bred, out of a bitch called Am. Ch. Laurwyn's Heywire Calliope CD. He became a Champion at eight months of age, by winning four majors in four shows, all from the puppy classes, in two weekends. In his first year, Baron was listed as the number four Wirehair and, by the time he was eighteen months old, he was a Group placing Wirehair. He was also NAVHDA tested by winning a second place. And he has sired several dogs who have been successful in both the field and the Obedience ring.

Am. Ch. Int. Ch. AfterHours Wyr'n Bo Jest is a son of Baron out of Am. Ch. Cassio Laurwyn's Crumb Cake, was bred by Walt and Tina Whitmore and is owned by Franz Neuwirth and Jean Renner. He too, like Baron, won his title by the time he was eight months of age, taking many Best of Breeds over the top Specials at the time. He has been in the top ten Wirehairs table every year since he was one year old. In 1992, when he was the number two Wirehair in the United States of America, his co-owner, Franz, took him to Europe, where he was a winner at the German Specialty show. He is also a Champion in Mexico and Costa Rica, making him an International Champion.

Am. Ch. AfterHours Electrick Outlet and Am. Ch. AfterHours Swedish Odyssey are half brother and sister, both being out of the Swedish imported bitch Mamba. Mamba's dam is Field Champion Luna and also included in her pedigree are Dual and Int. Ch. Addi and Int. Dual Ch. Karr.

Electrick Outlet, owned by Eileen Fahey, was Reserve Winners Bitch at the 1989 GWPCA National Specialty as a ten month old puppy. In addition to her show title, she has also won her CD title, and has an AKC Junior Hunter title and an AKC Good Citizen award. Her

Am. Ch./Int. Ch. AfterHours Wyr'n Bo Jest, owned by Franz Neuwirth and Jean Renner. A prolific winner in the show ring.

Am. Ch. AfterHours Electrick Outlet, owned by Eileen Fahey. Winner of the CD title and the AKC Junior Hunter title.

talents have not been restricted to bench and field activities, as she has also appeared on the television programme, 'Candid Camera'.

Swedish Odyssey was seven months old before he went to his new owner, Judy Parietti, who owns him in partnership with Tina Whitmore. Together they went to training classes until Judy gained enough confidence to take him into the show ring. At eleven months he won his first points from the puppy class and the following week-end he was awarded Best of Breed and collected a three point major. In his first Open class, he gained the Winners Dog and finished his title the following weekend, at the age of one year and two weeks of age, just six weeks after his first show. In the fall of 1992, at the GWPCA National Specialty, he won the Best of Opposite Sex in the Futurity. Swedish Odyssey is now concentrating on AKC Hunting tests, having already qualified for the first leg of the Junior

Hunter title. Am. Ch. AfterHours Spirit of Shurcan was bred by James and Barbara Halligan and Patricia Laurans and is sired by Am. Ch. Shurcan Baron of AfterHours out of Am. Ch. Laurwyn's Heywire Calliope CD, a product of a mother-to-son mating. She is a striking, white and liver bitch who helped to spark an interest in this unusual colour. She has produced five Am. Champions and is owned, in partnership, by Walt and Tina Whitmore and Christi Schoessow.

ASPENDEL: ROBERT PERRY

Aspendel was the kennel name of Robert Perry's Irish Setters and was used when the Wirehairs were introduced. Nearly twenty bench Champions are associated with the Aspendel prefix. The foundation Wirehair was the famous Am. Ch. Geronimo's Flying Warrior, who was owned by Dixie Perry and Cheryl Folendorf and bred by JoAnn Burns Steffes. He won seventeen Sporting Groups and the 1988 National Specialty from the Veteran class, in addition to several independent Specialties. He was the number one Wirehair in the breed points table for 1982, 1983, 1984 and 1985, and either number two or three Wirehair in the Group points table for 1983, 1984, 1985, 1986 and 1987. He has produced nearly forty Champions during a short stud career, having not been used at stud until he was four and a half years old.

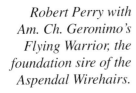

Robert Perry with Am. Ch. Geronimo's Flying Warrior, the foundation sire of the Aspendal Wirehairs.

Flying Warrior was used with Am. Ch. Weidenhugel O'Kim V. Gunner and the litter produced five Champions, including the youngest-ever Champion in America to finish her title, Am. Ch. Weidenhugel Vanessa Warrior, bred by Mildred Revell. She completed it at six months and three weeks of age in just seven shows.

Lady Katherine was a solid liver bitch, bred and owned by Marge and Gayle Armstrong, who won only thirteen show points, having never finished her title. But Lady Katherine produced nine Champions in just two litters, both sired by Flying Warrior. The most notable winner in her first litter was Am. Ch. C Wobegone Warrior. The repeat mating produced Am. Ch. Aspendel's L.J. Warrior D, who was the winner of the Puppy of the Year Tournament in the US. The prize, for Robert and Dixie Perry, was a visit to the UK for the Cruft's Dog Show in 1988.

Robert and Dixie divorced, but Robert has continued campaigning the Aspendel Wirehairs, including the top winning Am. Ch. C Wobegone Warrior. Wobe was the number one Wirehair in America in both breed and group points in 1988, 1989 and 1990. He is the winner of thirty-two Sporting groups, two all breed Best in Shows, and Best of Breed at the 1989 National Specialty, in addition to winning over 250 Best of Breeds. Wobe was brought out of retirement in 1993 and shown as a veteran. He still maintained his ability to win, with Best of Opposite Sex at the National Specialty and his second all breed Best in Show from the veteran classes.

Wobe's sister is Am. Ch. Cha Chas Warrior and she, too, has produced nine Champions. During her show career she won several Group placements and Best of Opposite Sex at the National Specialty in 1991, including winning the brood bitch class.

CADENBERG: SILKE ALBERTS

Silke Alberts emigrated from Germany to America in 1963. After attending a luncheon at Mildred Revell's Weidenbach kennels, Silke fell in love with a Wirehair there and booked a puppy from her litter. Unfortunately, the bitch puppy lacked the required furnishings and coat to be considered a true Wirehair. However, on vacation in Germany, Silke acquired Lutz Zur Cadenberg, barely six months of age, bred by Fritz Butt. Lutz began his show career when he was eighteen months old, and finished quickly, undefeated with twenty-one points, all majors. In the spring of 1976, he was entered in a fun field trial, with Silke knowing nothing about trials but just wanting to have a go. However, Lutz's natural ability shone and he went on to win the stake. Randy Berry was watching Lutz and offered to train him for some field trial work. This training was done over the weekends; one wonders what he would have been able to accomplish if he had received full-time training instead.

Lutz achieved his Amateur Field Championship in May 1977 and, five months later, he earned his finishing Open field point, qualifying for the title of Dual Ch. in October 1977. Despite an injury, he still managed to be an All-age dog in both 1978 and 1979. During 1979, he earned his Companion Dog Obedience title, and in 1982, aged ten, he earned his AKC Tracking dog title. Although entered in several Obedience Trials in the Open class, he was twice excused for limping after taking the jumps. He had, by then, developed arthritis and it was time for retirement.

Many of his progeny inherited his versatility. He produced Dual Ch. Flintlock's Not Too

Cadenberg Filou v Lutz CDX TD, on point, owned by Silke Alberts.

Shabby and Dual Ch./Am. Field Ch. Cadenberg Bacchanale v Lutz, both owned by Frank and Marion Fernandez. Field Ch./Am. Field Ch. Baron von Schyrental was bred by Klas Meyn out of a German import bitch Asta vom Schyrental and was owned by Mike Weatherton. Lutz has produced twenty-seven Champions and more than thirty-four NAVHDA Natural Ability tested dogs, with nineteen prize I, sixteen prize II and three prize III. In addition he has produced three NAVHDA Utility prize I, eight Utility prize II and seven Utility prize III. Two dogs have earned their AKC Tracking titles and Companion Dog Excellent Obedience Trials.

In 1992 he was chosen by the German Wirehaired Pointer Club of America to represent the breed in the American Kennel Gazette as an influential stud dog of the past.

Soon after acquiring Lutz, Silke purchased a bitch from Mildred Revell that turned out to be Am. Ch. Weidenhugel Capuccine CD TD, and she successfully achieved a NAVHDA Utility degree. The progeny Lutz and Cina have produced are exceptional, with great natural hunting instincts. Cina has produced eight Champions, one Amateur Field Champion, fifteen NAVHDA Natural Ability and one NAVHDA Utility dog. Cadenberg Filou v Lutz, CDX TD has a litter sister who has become a Dual Ch. Unfortunately Filou had an injury to her achilles tendon that prevented her from finishing her bench championship. She has a Utility NAVHDA Prize I, a CDX in Obedience and a TD in tracking. Filou is the mother of Dual & Amateur Field Ch. Cadenberg Magie v Rogue, who is a third generation Dual & Amateur Field Ch.

DC/AFC Cadenberg Magie v Rogue's sire is Dual Ch. Cascade Rogue, MH, and she thrives on working. She got all her points in the field in all-breed competitions and has always been in the top ten all-breed system results. Her awards are impressive and include AKC Canine good citizen, NAVHDA natural ability prize II, NAVHDA Utility test prize II, Herbst Zucht Prufung Prize I, and Wirehaired Pointing Griffon Test Natural Ability and Intermediate prize II.

CASCADE: RAY AND LYNN CALKINS

Ray and Lynn Calkins' emphasis has always been in the field and they state that, in their house, hunting is intense and performance is mandatory! When Ray decided that he wanted a hunting dog, he decided on a Wirehair and their first dog was a mail order special in 1974, called Drifter. It was a mutual learning experience so, when they received their first ribbon in his first field trial whilst still a puppy, they were well and truly hooked. His colour made him unusual and some trial judges referred to him as a "pointing sheep". There were few Wirehairs trialling in the northwest and the competition at the broke dog level was dominated by shorthairs and their professional handlers. However Drifter graduated to become Field Ch. Chancellor's Sierra Drifter at the prestigious East Seattle Pointer Club trial at the age of six years old.

In the meantime, Ray and Lynn had purchased a bitch of strong Haar Baron line's who was to become Am. Ch. Walkers Cascade Tess. Tess, mated to Drifter, produced the successful Wirehairs Dual Ch. Marsu's Sierra Cass and Dual Ch. Cascade Rogue, MH. Then she was mated to her father, American Ch. Fritz von Rank and produced Field Ch. & Amateur Field Ch. Cascade Steamer, MH, and Field Ch. Cascade Smokin' Jo, suitably named after Mount St Helens had erupted in May 1980.

DC Cascade Rogue, MH, finished his bench championship in 1980 and was moved to the field. Cade always preferred hunting to trialling and he hunted over all terrains and for all types of game, including the pointing of tortoises in the Mohave desert during the Master Hunter. His performance at the 1985 National Event gave him his Dual title and his National Open Title. Two years later he gained his National Amateur title at Assunpink in New Jersey. He was the first Dual of any breed to gain a prize in the NAVHDA utility test. Cade was not used extensively at stud, but he managed to produce Dual Ch./Am. Field Ch. Cadenberg Magie v Rogue and Dual Ch. Cascade Ike, MH.

FC Cascade Smokin' Jo was the star as a Puppy Derby dog and won the Futurity in 1982. His littermate, FC/AFC Cascade Steamer, MH, took over the limelight with all the talent of his dam, Tess. He was capable of running with any dog of any breed in America, using his uncanny nose and his amazing natural instincts. Without a doubt, he was the best trial dog that Ray and Lynn ever had the pleasure to train. He managed to clinch his Master Hunter,

Field Ch. Chancellor's Sierra Drifter, owned by Ray and Lynn Calkins, won his title at six years old.

Dual Ch. Cascade Rogue: This dog hunted over all terrains and for all types of game.

Dual Ch./Am. Field Ch. Cascade Ike, owned by Ray and Lynn Calkins. He is the kennel's current star.

and his National Amateur titles came in Branched Oak in 1985 and Fort Huachuca in 1986. He was bred to some very nice field Wirehairs and, to date, is the sire of five Field Champions. There are two other Wirehairs that have managed to sire five Field Champions and they are Herr Schmardt v Fox River and FC/AFC Halb von Pommoregon. Smokin' Jo has sired two Field Champions.

Dual Ch./Am. Field Ch. Cascade Ike, MH, is Ray and Lynn's present-day star. He was retained, until he was a year old, by his breeder who then found him too precocious to cope with, so he was offered for sale. After several callers had failed to look at him, it was suggested that Ray and Lynn would take him to evaluate and then to sell. On arrival, he was found to be a natural hunter with a tremendous nose and an unstoppable desire to please. Needless to say, he remained with Ray and Lynn. He won the National Title in 1991, which completed his field championship, and has gone on to be the Top All Breed Amateur Gun Dog in the Northwest in 1992. He finished his bench Championship and Amateur Field Championship in 1992, collecting his Master Hunter certificate also.

DESERT MILLS: HELEN SHELLEY

Helen Shelley's first Wirehair, Am. Ch. Mueller Mills Valentino, sired by Am. Ch. Oldmill's Casanova out of Mueller's Ina, was bred by Kurt Mueller. He had a spectacular show career, winning his show championship and the National Specialty in 1963 and repeating the National win in 1965. He also won seven all breed Best in Shows, eighty-eight group wins and one hundred and thirty-two placements.

Helen's Wirehairs have been based, primarily, on the Kurt Mueller dogs in addition to two German imports, both bitches, called Am. Ch. Ella v d Hohenroth and Britta von Landhaus.

Am. Ch. Mueller Mills Valentino II was, as his name suggests, a son of Helen's first Wirehair out of the German import Ella v d Hohenroth. He too was successful in the ring, winning his show championship in 1968 and following his father's achievement by winning a Best in Show all breeds. He accumulated thirty group wins and seventy placements during

Am. Ch. Mueller Mills Valentino II enjoyed a spectacular show career.

Am. Ch. Vodibar's Fanny Paltani, excelling in the field.

his career. Britta von Landhaus was bred to Am. Ch. Mueller Mills Valentino II twice and these became the foundation of the Desert Mills line. Am. Ch. Desert Mills Lon Chaney and Am. Ch. Desert Mills Medow Rok Willy are other Wirehairs who successfully gained their titles.

Recently Am. Ch. Vodibar's Fanny Paltani has been carrying the Desert Mills flag and is on her way to being Helen's first Dual Champion. Amongst her field wins were the GWPCA National Field Futurity in 1989 and fourth place in the 1993 GWPCA National Field Championship.

FLINTLOCKS: MIKE HEMPHILL

Mike Hemphill's first Wirehair was a bitch called Am. Ch. Dame Thecla who finished her title in five weeks. She produced a dog who won the Winners Dog at one of the Nationals and Dual Ch. Flintlocks Not too Shabby, sired by DC/AFC Lutz zur Cadenberg, who was a winner of the Open Gundog at the GWPCA National Field Trial in California during 1981.

Dual Ch. Flintlocks Medicine Man, bred by Mike and sired by FC/AFC Fredrich's Figure it Out, out of Flintlock's Bushwacker, has hunted every legal game in the Western part of America, including successfully following blood trails. He has also never failed to retrieve, whether it has been on land or in water.

ALOYSIA HARD

Aloysia's first Wirehair was a dog born in 1979 and was by Am. Ch. Aramis V Beau out of Heidi von Hohenzollern. He became the illustrious Am., Dutch and VDH Champion Weidenhugel Moonraker. When Aloysia moved to Germany in 1983 she took Moonraker with her. He was already an American Champion and had won several group placements. He was entered at Dortmund for the German Republic National Championships show, along with the top winning German exhibits and, to the surprise of everyone, ended up as being the Bundessieger (Best of Breed). The Bundessieger is only awarded if the individual dog has been given a Vorzuglich (superior) rating. Much to the Germans' surprise and to Aloysia's pleasure, he repeated this prestigious feat in 1984, 85 and 86. What a tremendous achievement for an American-bred Wirehair to win this award in the Wirehair's Country of origin!

Moonraker also added the awards of Europasieger 1985, Weltsieger 1985 and Brno Sieger 1985. Additionally, he won places in many groups both in Germany and Holland, including winning a group at Dortmund in 1985 and a Reserve Best in Show in Stuttgart.

When Aloysia returned from Germany in 1988 she brought with her two Wirehairs from Italy. These are Am. Ch. Ali del Chisola and Am. Ch. Alfa del Chisola, both by Brutus del Chisola. Having been extremely impressed with the quality, good nature, non-aggressive temperament and working ability of these two Wirehairs, Aloysia imported a third Italian Wirehair in 1990 called Pola del Chisola, sired by Notus del Chisola.

Ali began his field trial work in 1991 and, handled by Aloysia, has half the points necessary for his Field Trial Championship. In the spring of 1992, he was ranked number five on the top ten list, which is based on both wins and placements in the field. Unfortunately he was unable to compete that autumn because of illness but, despite this, he finished in tenth place. He completed his show championship in 1992. One of Ali's sons, called Piemonte Gianni v. Chisola, is already winning in the show ring and has begun his

Am. Dutch and VDH Ch. Weidenhugel Moonraker, owned by Aloysia Hard. This American-bred Wirehair won Best of Breed (Bundessieger) for four successive years in Germany.

Fox & Cook

field work. Alfa won her show championship easily, collecting Best of Winners at the National Specialty show at 18 months of age and finishing with major wins by the age of two years. She, too, began her field trial work in 1991 and has also featured in the top ten list. Aloysia handles her in the Californian trials, but for most of the field trial season she is handled by Mike Hemphill of the Flintlock Kennels.

HEYWIRE: JUDY CHESHIRE

Judy Cheshire has been involved with Wirehairs for over twenty years and owes a great deal to both Pat Laurans and Betty Stroh for being her teachers and mentors. Judy's main interests are the conformation shows and Obedience Trials, although she does have Wirehairs with Field Trial placements. Her location and limited free time restrict her involvement in the field work.

The first Wirehair that Judy ever saw was Am. Ch. Hilltop's SS Cheesecake CD, the top winning Wirehair bitch in the history of the breed in America. Judy's first introduction to Wirehairs was through a daughter of Cheesecake, Am. Ch. Laurwyn's Cream Cheese. She produced a litter, sired by Am. Ch. Hilltop's Bradshaw, and it was from this that Judy chose her foundation bitch, who became Am. Ch. Laurwyn's Brie CD.

Brie was bred only twice. Once, linebred to Am. Ch. Laurwyn's Cheese Cobbler, she produced Am. Ch. Laurwyns Heywire Calliope CD, who was the dam of Am. Ch. Shurcan Baron of AfterHours. Her second litter was to Am. Ch. Johmar's Justin Tyme. She produced an all breed Best in Show winning bitch, called Am. Ch. Heywire's Happily Ever After CD, and a High-in-Trial winner at the 1987 GWPCA National Specialty, Am. Ch. Heywire's Always a Bridesmaid CD.

Bridesmaid was bred once to Am. Ch. Laurwyn's Cheeseburger and produced five bench Champions. They included Am. Ch. Heywire's Wynfall O'Shadra CD, MH, who won the Winners Bitch at the 1987 National Specialty and Am. Ch. Heywire's Windstorm, who won the Best in Sweepstakes at the same National Specialty and is now a narcotics dog with a state police department. Another littermate was Heywire's Woodwind, who won the Puppy

Am. Ch. Heywire's Happily Ever After CD, owned by Helen Shelley, Beverly Murray and Judy Cheshire.

Classic at the same 1987 National Specialty. Judy has been active in the GWPCA as Secretary, and also in other capacities.

INVERNESS: LAURA AND JACK MYLES

Laura and Jack Myles established the Inverness Kennels in 1979, with the aim of producing all-round working Wirehairs. They strongly believe that the Wirehair is extremely versatile, so their dogs have been, and continue to be, nationally ranked in both the Obedience and the breed rings. They also continue to breed close-working gundogs for foot hunter use. Laura is a certified Senior Judge in National Shoot to Retrieve, NASTRA, and she also Judges AKC Field Trial Stakes and AKC Hunting dog tests.

Am. & Can. Dual Champion Fredrichs Vogel Jaeger: One of only two Wirehairs that are Dual Champions in both America and Canada. Owned by Jack and Laura Myles and Paul Fredrich.

Am. Ch. Spindrifters Mark of Laurwyn: A multiple Specialty winner, he was the result of a mating between a top show bitch and a top field dog.

Can. Ch. Hennum's Duchess Wilhelm, CD, was their first Wirehair. She was a gift from Laura's parents, Ray and Mae Hennum, and is considered one of the best dogs they have owned. She was born in 1977 by Am. & Can. Ch. Odell's Hansel, CDX, out of Am. Ch. Wildfire's That Girl, who was from German stock. She was a personal foot hunting dog, who particularly loved to hunt ducks out of a blind, and would sit listening to the ducks calling to each other long before they came into gun range. She whelped two litters, both by Am. and Can. Ch. Hennum's Baron Wilhelm, UD, and she produced five Champions.

The Myles co-owned Am. & Can. Dual Ch. Fredrichs Vogel Jaeger, with Paul Fredrich. Buster is one of the only two Wirehairs to date that have been credited with becoming both a show and a field Ch. in both the United States and Canada. He was a tall, rangy, gentle clown who was an excellent big running All-Age dog. He was hunted mostly on chukar and pheasants, but would work close and hunt ducks when asked. For a predominately field dog, he did surprisingly well in the show ring and was Winner Dog and Best of Winners at a local Specialty in 1990. Buster was an all-round dog, willing to participate in whatever he was asked to.

Am. Ch. Rex Von Soyen, from the Weidenhugel lines, was OFA clear for Hip Dysplasia. Originally a poor rescue dog, he soon settled and became a decent show dog. He had a short tight coat, with a masculine body, and big driving movement.

Fredrich's Liesel V Inverness, born in 1989, is Laura's personal hunting dog. She is a niece to Dual Ch. Fredrichs Vogel Jaeger. Liesel's sire is Field Ch. Cascade Steamer, MH, who is a top field dog from the Calkins kennel. Her dam is Dual Ch. Fredrich's Rosy Bear, who was Winners Bitch at the Nebraska Nationals. Liesel is a smallish bitch, with a short tight coat and a short beard. She is stylish on point,with a very good nose, and she is about to commence her second year of solid hunting on pheasant and quail. Liesel has produced a litter by Am. Dual Ch. Cascade Ike, MH. She has also successfully completed the AKC Hunting test requirements for the Junior Hunter level.

Am. Ch. Spindrifters Mark of Laurwyn was born in 1981 and bred by John Writer. Mark was a result of a mating between the top show bitch Am. Can. Ch. Laurwyns Barbed Wire and the top field dog Am. & Can. Dual Ch. and Amateur Field Ch. Nordwest's Griff Von Dem Feld, CD. Mark is a willing, eager-to-please dog, who has passed these characteristics on and produced sensible working gundogs. Mark has a true, correct wire coat that is able to shed water and feels like a wire brush. In the show ring he has been very successful, becoming a multiple Specialty Winner.

Am. Ch. Inverness Just in Time, JH, was born in 1983 and was out of Am. Can. Ch. Inverness Bianca. Justin was a medium-sized dog, with tremendous drive and movement. He was Winners Dog at the 1983 Nationals out of the six to nine month class, was NAVHDA Natural Ability rated, earned a Junior Hunter title, and finished his bench championship. He had been successfully used at stud and produced progeny with Hunting titles, Obedience titles and conformation points.

JAMAR: MARILYN AND HERB POWELL

Marilyn and Herb Powell first became interested in purebred dogs in late 1974 and they owned, bred and field-trialled Irish Setters. Through a field trainer, they became aware of the Wirehairs and acquired their first one in 1977, named Ch. Jamars Schinken v Whitewings. She was bred by Maury Smith out of a German imported bitch Arni V.D. Haid. Their first litter was in the spring of 1979, between Am. Ch. Desert Mills Lon Chaney and Am. Ch. Jamars Schinken V Whitewings. To date, Marilyn and Herb have produced nine litters, containing numerous bench champions, Junior Hunter titles and wonderful hunting companion dogs.

Am. Ch. Jamar's Oh Henry started at six months of age by picking up a five point major and Best of Opposite in Sweepstakes at the Southern California Specialty. He followed that by winning Reserve Winners Dog and Best in Sweeps at the Nationals in 1988. He finished

Am. Ch. Jamars Hot Pursuit: A successful representative from Marilyn and Herb Powell's Jamar kennel.

his title with two more majors and two Best of Breeds. He then progressed into the Specials ring, and by the age of two he was a multiple group winner and placer, with two Specialties under his belt. His son, Am. Ch. Jamar's Back in Time, also finished in style, with his third Best of Breed and a Group 3.

KOOPMAN'S

John Koopman's first Wirehairs were purchased for hunting and as companions in 1985. In 1986 he imported two Wirehairs from Holland, one of which was used as a foundation for the line. He was called Colt v.d. Pijnhorst and was by Dutch Field Trial Ch. Quell v.d. Wupperaue out of a bitch called Kim.

John's primary purpose is to produce top-quality hunting and companion dogs, with a high degree of natural ability for use in both land and water. He wants his dogs to have conformation as close to the breed standard as possible, with hard, flat-lying coats which do not require any stripping or clipping. Although the Koopman Wirehairs are basically hunting dogs, John has entered, and been successful, at some shows in Canada even though the breed is not yet very popular, and entries are few. His Wirehairs hunt, during the autumn, on all upland game birds and waterfowl and turn to field trials during the spring. John's Wirehairs are very competitive in both NSTRA and Canadian Kennel Club trials.

Colt v.d. Pijnhorst passed his field dog test with a very high score. In addition, during 1992, whilst only entered in the spring season trials, he still became Canada's Number One Wirehair in Amateur Shooting dog competitions and Number Nine for all pointing breeds.

NORDIC RUNS: RAY AND MAE HENNUM

Ray and Mae Hennum have owned Wirehairs since 1976. After seeing a Wirehair working outstandingly in the field, Ray contacted Dick and Bonnie Larson in Seattle, and he and Mae became the owners of a Wirehair who grew up to become Am. & Can. Ch. Hennums Baron Wilhelm UD.

Willy achieved his Am. Ch. title in 1979, his Can. Ch. title in 1980 and, in 1981, he became the second dog to earn a Utility Obedience title in the United States. To prove his versatility, at the Seattle Kennel Club show on August 5th 1979 he received a qualifying score towards his CD title, took Best of Breed out of a good entry, and went on to take first place in the Sporting Group.

Willy actually did not start his Obedience work until he was more than three and half years old. His progression was quick, and he only took eighteen months to achieve his Utility degree from the time he received his CD title.

Willie was retired from the show ring after the Monroe show, when he had taken Best of Breed, and his daughter was Best of Opposite Sex. One of his daughters was to become Laura Myles' companion whilst she was at University and she became Am. Can. Ch. Inverness Nordic Brandy UD.

In 1981 they purchased a two year old bitch from Flip Bowser, who was the progeny of German imports. She became Am. Ch. Astra vom Viking CD and produced two litters. From her last litter, Ray and Mae retained a bitch puppy and named her Brandy. She has gone on to become Am. Can. Ch. OTCH Nordics Viking Brandy, Can. CDX. She won her

The first Obedience Trial Champion in America, Am. & Can. OTCH. Nordics Viking Brandy, owned by Ray and Mae Hennum.

American title in 1988 and her Canadian title in 1990. Her most notable achievement is that of being the first German Wirehaired Pointer ever to win an Obedience trial champion title in the United States of America. This she did at the Seattle KC show on August 2nd 1992.

One of her notable successes has been in achieving High-in-Trial at the Washington State Obedience training clubs' Seattle show, with a score of 197.5 out of a possible 200, beating 264 dogs. Also, in Canada, she gained another High-in-Trial, with a perfect score of 200. Over her Obedience career, Brandy has accumulated seventeen High-in-Trial, as well as a number of Best of Breed wins.

To date Ray has handled three Wirehairs to their Utility degrees – quite an achievement.

SGR: SUZANNE RICHARDSON

SGR stands for Suzanne Gail Richardson, who owns the dogs that come under this kennel name. Gail's first Wirehair was Am. Ch. Bach v Schnellberg and he was purchased in 1981 as a six week old puppy. He was an excellent gun dog and was hunted extensively, never seeming to tire. He was put to Gail's second Wirehair, Schnellberg's Vanilla Mousse and was linebred Schnellberg. At the time, her white colour was being frowned upon and, although she got both her Majors, she was retired to the whelping box.

This litter produced the Dual Ch. SGR Silent Running, CD, MH. Known as Levi, he was one of eleven puppies, born on a cold December 15th 1985. The combination of his unique colour and his bold, confident personality, made the choice of retaining him easy. He was considered a large puppy and slow to mature. However, now fully grown, he stands twenty-five and a half inches high. As a puppy, he ran only once and he was placed fourth in a two-point puppy stake. The following spring he was turned over to professional trainer, Jim Basham.

He took his first show point at eleven months and then was not shown again for seven months. On his return to the show ring, and in a span of four weeks, he accumulated nine points. He was then returned to Jim Basham in preparation for the Nationals. He went on to win several Derby placements before going second in the 1987 National Derby and winning the Futurity. Levi went home on November 1st and, back in the show ring, added a four-point major to these accomplishments. He ended the year by being number six GWPCA Puppy/Derby dog.

In 1988 he accumulated ten points from gun dog stakes and topped the year off by finishing fourth in the National Championships. At under three years of age he was the youngest finalist. Overall, he was the number five GWPCA Gun Dog for 1988 and, additionally, won another nine points towards his bench title.

In the spring of 1989, at the first trial of the season, Levi injured his foot severely. Even though his foot was badly cut, his determined character meant that his injury was not noticed until after the trial, where he had managed to be awarded third place. Later that spring, when he was able to move soundly again, he returned to the ring and completed his bench championship. Even though, in 1989, due to his injury, he only competed for half the season, he still managed to end up again as number five GWPCA Gun Dog. Early in 1990, he set the tone for the coming year by winning second from an entry of thirty-seven in an open dog stake at Killdeer Plains, Ohio. He completed his Field title in October 1990, and

Dual Ch. SGR Silent Running, owned by Gail Richardson.

had five Amateur points and four consecutive qualifying Master Hunter scores.

He has produced six bench Champions and is currently the second top producer of titled Hunting test dogs. He is the youngest sire with a Master to his credit, and that is SGR Silent Knight, MH, who finished at twenty-five months old. Levi is also one of only three Wirehairs who hold both a Dual title and a Master Hunting title. In 1989, Gail purchased a bitch puppy from John Scoonover, because she had been very impressed with the dam, Field Ch./Am. Field Ch. Marie Laveau Von Steuben. Brew turned out to be Field Ch. SGR Witches' Brew, completing her field title at twenty-six months of age, and also winning the National Field Futurity in the same year.

SOO LINE: ELIZABETH BARRETT

A very active person, at both national and local level, is Elizabeth Barrett. Her first Wirehair was a rescue case, and not a great representative of the breed, eleven years ago. In 1984 Elizabeth contacted Diana Nordrum and Bob Calentine and bought a bitch puppy. She turned out to be Am. Ch. Liebenwaid's Doc's Drieka, SH. Her talents included Field Trial placements in juvenile stakes, Senior Hunter and her bench championship. She also won the brood bitch class at the 1987 Nationals in New Jersey. Her litter, to Am. Ch. Geronimo's Flying Warrior, produced eleven puppies, one of which was Am. Ch. Liebenwaid's War's Razzmatazz, who only requires two more legs for his Senior Hunting degree. When he finishes that, it means there will be three generations of Senior Hunters in Elizabeth's line.

Am. Ch. Dana Nordica's A Victor was imported from Denmark. Duly impressed with this blood line, Elizabeth decided to import a bitch from Denmark. Having made this decision

The Danish import Danske Fie sitting, and Am. Ch. Soo Line's Lil Abner standing, on rocks on Lake Superior, Wisconsin; owned by Elizabeth Barrett.

Pheasant hunting in North Dakota, Elizabeth Barrett pictured with her Wirehair family.

Elizabeth, together with some friends, went there on a visit. The dog whose bloodlines particularly interested her was the number one Wirehair in Denmark, Dk.Ch. Int.Ch. Dk.JCH. Aakjaer's Plet, who is the first Wirehair to have what is the equivalent to a Dual Championship. She returned to America with the bitch puppy, Danske Fie, who is just one point short on her bench championship, but already has Field Trial placements in juvenile stakes. Am. Ch. Soo Line's Lil Abner is out of Elizabeth's foundation bitch, Am. Ch Liebenwaid's Doc's Drieka by the Danish dog Am. Ch. Dana Nordica's A Victor. Although he has Field Trial placements, he has been more impressive in Hunt Tests and has two legs towards his Master Hunter title. His brother, Soo Line's Allied Freighter, has achieved puppy and Derby points in the field, including First in the puppy classes at the 1990 Nationals, and is close to getting his show championship.

Most of Elizabeth's help on the field side has come from the experienced trainer, Jim Basham. Various methods are used to keep her dogs fit for competing in field events. In the spring and summer they are exercised behind either a bike or her horses, and in the winter they are harnessed up to a sled.

VON DUFFIN: TERRY AND ANN DUFFIN

The Von Duffin kennels are owned by Terry and Ann Duffin, who have owned Wirehairs for twelve years. Having bred for disposition and hunting ability, in addition to conformation and coat, they owned the 1991 National Field Futurity Winner, Cascade Liebchen Von Duffin, who unfortunately died soon after. Recently they won the 1993 National Specialty Best of Breed with Am. Ch. Cascade Cate Von Duffin SH, who is a daughter of NFC/DC Cascade Rogue MH. Cate won her Senior Hunter before she was two and is fully broke to wing and shot. She began her career as a Special in July 1993 and has since won over thirty Best of Breeds, a Group One, two Group Two and a Group Three.

Am. Ch. Cascade Cate Von Duffin winning the 1993 National Specialty, owned by Terry and Ann Duffin.

Booth.

Chapter Nine

THE WIREHAIR WORLDWIDE

AUSTRALIA

The first German Wirehaired Pointer arrived in Australia in late 1976. He was dog called Wittekind Amigo, who was imported from Britain by Mr W. Krahnen. During the following year, Mr Krahnen also imported a bitch, Wittekind Britt. As their names reveal, they came from the first two litters bred by Mieneke Mills de Hoog. Unfortunately, no records have been found to indicate that either the dog or bitch were ever shown or trialled and they do not appear in any of the pedigrees of the current stock in Australia.

Two years later, in 1978, three bitches and a dog arrived. Dawsons Secret Storm came from New Zealand and went to the Korskote kennels of Anne Atkinson, Wittekind Cleo from Britain went to Geoff Oakes' Ostoja kennels, and Wittekind Dubbeltje, from the same source, Mieneke Mills de Hoog, went to the Westerwald kennels. These bitches laid the foundation for the breed in Australia. The dog, called Dawsons Cracklin' Jack, who was Secret Storm's brother, was imported by Kim Mansbridge but was not used for breeding.

1979 saw the arrival of litter brothers from New Zealand, Dawsons Barbed Wire, who also went to the Korskote kennels, and Dawsons Biff Bangabird, for Ostoja. Later on in 1979 the Westerwald kennels imported a dog from New Zealand, called Dawsons Hot Wire, and the Ostoja kennels brought in a bitch called Dawsons Diamond Lil from New Zealand and a dog named Wittekind Special Agent from Britain. All the British imports to arrive in Australia were direct descendants of the early Dutch imports to the UK. Consequently, Australia was in the same situation as had existed there, with the Wirehairs all related, so breeding was restricted and the breed was slow in developing.

It was not until late 1984 that a new bloodline was introduced. This was a bitch called Tickencote Sail Away, who was again imported from the UK. More followed. A dog who became Terrington Boy of Korskote followed from Great Britain in 1987, Dawson Carl was imported by the Kobnko kennels from New Zealand in 1988, and in 1989 Aggie Vom Bischoff was imported by the Korskote kennels from New Zealand. These later imports were, however, also directly from the foundation British stock. Then in 1990 a dog was imported from Sweden. He was called Frost and was brought in by John Blomstedt. The most recent increase in the gene pool has been a litter produced in February 1993 as a result of artificial insemination. The semen was imported from the United States of America, from

Aust. Ch. Dawsons Secret Storm, the first Wirehair Champion in Australia, owned by Anne Atkinson.

the sire Am. Ch. Weidenhugel Intrepid V Goetz. The number of Wirehairs has doubled in the past few years, although it is still small, possibly less than one hundred throughout Australia. Very few are seen at field or retrieving trials, but they are making their presence known in the show ring, in obedience and in agility trials. It is hoped that the breed will become as popular in Australia as it is in other countries in the near future.

KOBNKO: TRISH BOND

Trish Bond from Queensland, who owns the Kobnko Wirehairs, was living in New Zealand in 1978 when she acquired her first Wirehair, having seen the picture of one in a book. This was a bitch, who became Ch. Dawsons Joy-D-Vere, sired by Basco v.d. Andesheim out of Ch. Dawsons Aquarius. She won two Best Baby in Show awards and two Best Puppy in Group wins. Three months later, Trish purchased her half-sister, Dawsons Kween, who was out of Alice of Kenstaff. Joy-D-Vere produced two litters, but unfortunately only one litter survived. Two of these were titled and two others bought purely for hunting.

When Trish moved to Australia she purchased a bitch called Korskote Frei, whose life was tragically cut short by a car accident. Fortunately she had also bought another Wirehair, from Jack Dawson, who became Aust. Ch. Dawsons Carl. Carl sired one litter and that was to an unshown bitch called Korskote Bianca V Borste. From it came Kobnko Boy Blazer, who was shown and field trialled in Western Australia, and two bitches retained by Trish called Kobnko Back to Back and Kobnko Bessie Be Mine. Both were successfully shown, with Back to Back winning forty-eight CCs. Carl has been a good winner in the show ring despite only appearing there for two years. He has won two Baby in Show, three Open and one runner-up in show. He has now been semi-retired from the show ring.

Trish's recent star is Korskote Touch N Go, who is one of the litter sired by Am. Ch. Weidenhugel Intrepid V Goetz by AI. Touch N Go has been shown eight times, has won three Baby in Shows, seven Baby in Groups, one minor in Group, and one Champion puppy in Group, gaining his first Challenge along the way.

Aust. Ch. Dawsons Carl, owned by Trish Bond.

KORSKOTE: ANNE ATKINSON

The Korskote German Wirehaired Pointers are owned by Anne Atkinson of Wilberforce, New South Wales. Anne's first Wirehair, in January 1978, was the bitch puppy from Jack Dawson of New Zealand. The progeny of two British imports, NZ Ch. Wittekind Auslage and Alice of Kenstaff, this puppy went on to become Australian Ch. Dawsons Secret Storm and was to be the first Wirehair there to gain her conformation title, in November 1978.

In early 1980, Secret Storm was sent to New Zealand to be mated with another British import, NZ Ch. Basco v.d. Andesheim. This litter produced two Champions. One was Aust. Ch. Korskote Behende, owned by Mr C. Ericksson, who was also the first Australian Wirehair to win at a retrieving trial. The second Champion was Aust. Ch. Korskote Borste, who was Australia's first Wirehair to achieve Best in Show at an all-breed Championship show, which he won in February 1983. The need for new bloodlines led to Tickencote Sail Away being imported from Britain in 1984. Sail Away had three litters by Borste and they produced a Dual Champion and six Australian Champions, of which four are multiple In Group winners and one has gained a CD title.

The most recent success for Anne and the Korskote Wirehairs was when, after a number of attempts, a litter was produced in February 1993 by artifical insemination with frozen semen imported from the Weidenhugel Kennels in America. The dam, Korskote Briana V Borste, was surgically inseminated with semen from Am. Ch. Weidenhugel Intrepid V Goetz and produced nine puppies.

By the time that the litter was seven months of age, four of the puppies had already won major prizes in the show ring. Korskote Touch of Klass and Korskote Touch of Magik, retained by Anne, Korskote Touch N Go, owned by Trish Bond from the Kobnko Kennels, and Korskote Touch of Style, owned by Mr and Mrs D. Matthews, have already achieved In Group wins and points towards their Championship title. Touch N Go's record to date is eight In Group wins from eight shows.

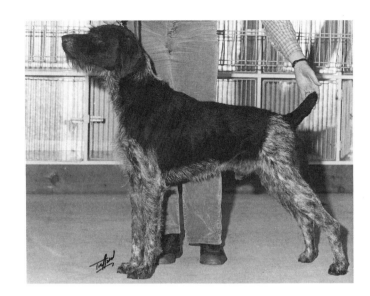

Aust. Ch. Korskote Borste, Australia's first all breeds Best in Show Winner, owned and bred by Anne Atkinson.

Michael Trafford.

OSTOJA: GEOFF OAKES

The Ostoja kennel, owned by Geoff Oakes in Cockatoo Valley, South Australia, was one of the early importers of Wirehairs, bringing in the bitch Wittekind Cleo, who was the first Wirehair in that part of the country, the dog Wittekind Special Agent, together with Dawsons Biff Bangabird and Dawsons Diamond Lil.

The most notable Wirehair owned by Geoff was the Dual Champion Dawsons Biff Bangabird. He gained his conformation title in 1981 and, in May 1983, attained his Utility Field Trial title to become Australia's first Field titled and Dual Champion Wirehair. Biffy also competed in one other event, a retrieving trial, when he was about six years old. He won that but, because of Geoff's commitments, did not continue to compete in retrieving trials. He was, however, used as a rough shooter's dog until his death in 1991. Biffy worked in Western Australia, South Australia, Victoria and New South Wales, so his ability in the field was widely known.

NEW ZEALAND

The Wirehair was introduced into New Zealand by Jack Dawson, who imported a dog and a bitch – Wittekind Auslage and Alice of Kenstaff from England in the early 1970s, followed by another dog, Baron VD Andesheim. The first two Field Trial Champions were bred by Jack Dawson, and they were Dawsons Arabesque and Dawsons Tabek. Both of these two Wirehairs are owned and trialled by Alf Shepherd from Auckland, and have achieved major success.As the New Zealand Field trial regulations have no separate categories for HPR breeds, the Wirehairs have to compete against Pointers and Setters, in addition to HPRs.

FT Ch. Dawsons Arabesque won the New Zealand Pointer Setter Championship when she was seven years old, together with many Club Championships and a North Island Championship. Alf has always given commands to his Wirehairs in Maori, so that nobody

NZ Ch. Wiggmansburg Amigo: Imported from the UK.

else can use the same commands. Further imports came from England, namely Dawsons English Connection, imported by Jack Dawson, and NZ Ch. Wiggmansburg Amigo, imported by Mark Somers.

The Wirehair has been quickly accepted into New Zealand, although the breed is still small in numbers with only three to four litters being registered each year. However, Wirehairs are capable of giving a good account of themselves on all manner of game, and consequently they have gained a strong following in Southland. A Southlander professional deer hunter called Bob Bragg managed in just nineteen days to recover seventy-four deer, with the help of two Wirehairs.

KOPFJAGER: PENNY TONKIN

Penny Tonkin purchased her first Wirehair in 1987, from Mr P. Geary in Mataura, New Zealand. The cute, hairy bundle called Ewok started his show career at the Tux National Dog show by winning Best Puppy in Breed, beating the English import, Wiggmansburg Amigo. The subsequent pictures were shown on television national news that night. From this impressive start, he became NZ Ch. Geardale Borage and was shown thirty-five times, taking the CC and Best of Breed every time, in addition to winning Best Intermediate in Show at the CGDS Specialty show in 1989.

Penny's next acquisition was the Australian import, Korskote Just Oki. She, too, gained her show title and was the only Wirehair to win Best of Breed over Ewok. Oki had, until her

Kopfjager Polar Wind, owned by Mr B. Railton, taking the easy option returning from the bush after deer stalking.

subsequent progeny was shown, never been beaten for the CC or Best of Breed. Oki has also taken a Best Junior in Show under Gundog specialist Mr W. Chambers.

Both Ewok and Oki enjoy working. Ewok prefers to hunt, using his excellent nose, rather than showing, with Oki backing him up and excelling in water retrieves. This combination of looks and ability has been passed on to their progeny. Although Kopfjager Icebird has been shown only twice, she has won one Baby Puppy in Group and one Bitch CC. Kopfjager Icehawk, shown five times, has won five Dog CCs and five Best of Breeds. Kopfjager Snowfalcon is Penny's field dog, who has gained a reputation for tenacity when going through gorse to track and recover pheasants and an ability to hear ducks well before they approach the shooters, allowing time for everybody to be alert.

Ewok and Oki's progeny's temperament and good looks have impressed many who have seen them. However, to Penny they are just family dogs, and future plans are to continue having puppies they are happy with. Penny has not set out to win everything but rather to enjoy her Wirehairs and, perhaps, improve the breed, particularly regarding temperament.

DAVID McDERMOTT

David has had Wirehairs for nine and a half years and his first was a bitch called Dawsons Pico. Unfortunately her temperament towards strangers left a bit to be desired. So, even though she had won the Otago Pointer and Setter Championship in 1986, David and his wife made the hard decision to sell her to a more suitable home.

NZ Ch. Korskote Hot Wyre, owned by David McDermott. 'Mac' recovered from terrible injuries to resume his Field Trial career.

Then, in December 1986, they collected Korskote Hot Wyre from the airport, who had been sent over by Anne Atkinson from Australia. David enjoyed gundog trialling, so it was important for his Wirehair to be trained for field work. Mac, as he was known, had his first gundog trial at the Southland Club and his first event was the puppy water, which he went on to win. So David entered him in the Novice Range and Find and, out of fourteen dogs competing, Mac finished third. By the end of 1987, Mac's gundog trialling was successful and it resulted in him winning the Aggregate Cup for the puppy section of the Southland Club. In addition to this, he came tenth in the New Zealand Pointer and Setter Championship at Western Southland. The 1988 trialling season started well, with a third-equal placing at the South Otago Pointer and Setter Championship, a first in the Novice at the Otago Championship, and a third in the Western Southland Pointer and Setter Championship.

This all came to an end on March 22nd. During the evening Mac escaped and was hit by a car. David rushed him to the vet, to be told that he had got bad bruising but would be alright. The following night, although he was still moving around, Mac was in extreme discomfort ,so David returned to the vet and asked for an X-ray. This showed that Mac had broken his neck.

Collett Brick, from a veterinary clinic in Invercargill, anaesthetized Mac to investigate the damage. Between the first two vertebrae she found two fractures and a gap. By this stage, Mac had deteriorated, and it was decided to fly him to Christchurch for emergency surgery by a specialist veterinary orthopaedic surgeon. Despite the knowledge that success was in considerable doubt, the operation took place. Mac's recovery was long and slow, yet he showed daily progress. After a lot of intensive care, he was able to stand with the aid of a support, and then graduated to being able to walk with the help of a sling suspended from a clothes-line.

Helmsley Miss Chief pointing quail with NZ Ch. Korskote Hot Wyre backing.

On April 11th David collected Mac, who was still only able to push up his front two legs and sit on his haunches. Just four days later he managed to walk six steps, a demonstration of his determination. In less than a month he was walking again, still unsteady but improving slowly. Then he was back working in the field, though care was taken not to ask too much of him. He competed in the Southland Novice Range and Find and managed to win the trial. The highlight of his trialling career was at the Southland Pointer and Setter Championship. He gained second-equal, just three points behind the winner.

Mac's remarkable recovery after his accident enabled him to achieve his final breed CCs to become a New Zealand Champion. Then a year later Mac experienced problems which required more surgery and a course of steroids. But since then he has never looked back, is still working in the field and has been able to sire three litters of puppies, albeit by AI. From the first litter, David acquired a bitch. She is called Helmsley Miss Chief, and is proving to be an excellent worker. From his second litter a dog puppy, exported to Harje and Christina Thunholm in Sweden, is also working exceptionally well.

HOLLAND

VAN DE BEMMERAUE: ROB JAGERSZKY

Rob Jagerszky started in 1970 with gundogs, acquiring first an Irish Setter and then a Gordon Setter, but he finally decided that neither of them was physically capable of doing the real fieldwork he wanted. So, in 1974, he bought his first Wirehair. She was Tanja v.d. Gender. Rob, however, felt that the quality of the breed at that time still left something to be desired. With Tanja he won quite a few matches, amongst them the Grote Flevo Polder in 1978, which is where the best gundogs from Holland compete. Tanja was also successful in Field Trials. Due to a combination of Tanja successes and, more important, the efforts of the

Rob Jagerszky's German import, Dutch Field Trial Champion Quell V.D. Wupperaue: This dog had a major impact on the breeding scene in Holland.

Chairman of the VVDD, Mr A.J. van Buuren, the breed started to become more prominent.

Rob then became interested in acquiring a faster dog and contacted the Wupperaue kennels in Germany. He bought Quell V.D. Wupperaue, who became a Dutch Field Trial Champion. Quell was sixty-three centimetres high and gained a top grade for show conformation. Rob states that he was not afraid of anything and, being his own man, was a born leader. He also had a major impact on the breeding scene in Holland. He fathered a great many beautiful, good dogs and was considered to be the Wirehair who made the Dutch dogs quicker and more elegant in their working. Quell also improved the coats in the Dutch Wirehairs.

To help form the foundation of the van de Bemmeraue kennels, Rob purchased Ester from Mawa's Home and Basko Von Steinbergen Wald to use with Quell's progeny. Rob considers that one of the best litters he bred was from a Quell daughter, called Gonny v.d. Bemmeraue, to Basko. Out of this litter came both Sjors and Vita v.d. Bemmeraue, who have collected many qualifications at Field trials, thus proving their natural characteristics. Currently Rob has progeny from Vita by the other Dutch International Working Champion, Heioord's Dracon, who is owned by Mr Bolle.

ITALY

DEL CHISOLA: ERNESTO ZACCO

In common with most European Countries, the Italian Wirehairs more usually compete in Field trials. One of the most famous Italian kennels belongs to Ernesto Zacco, who began with Wirehairs about twenty years ago with the initial intention of showing them. However, he quickly became interested in Field Trials. The most famous del Chisola Wirehair is Italian and International Field Ch. Brutus del Chisola, who won the World Field Trial Championship, in Holland, during 1984 and again in 1987, in Germany, against all HPRs.

Italian and Int. Field Trial Ch. Brutus del Chisola, winner of the World Field Trial Championship in 1984 and 1987, owned and bred by Ernesto Zacco.

Brutus's breeding goes back in the third generation to primarily Yugoslavian breeding on one side and Italian and German on the other.

Another well-known dog was Italian and International Field Champion Cris del Chisola. In addition to these two successful field dogs, Ernesto Zacco has bred Italian Field Champions Leda del Chisola, Arras v.d. Masch and Italian Show and Field Champion Ali.

Sr Zacco's kennels are impressive, because of the facilities and the excellent quality of his dogs. Most of them are solid dark liver with good coats The temperament and character of the del Chisola Wirehairs are self-evident, as in many of the runs he will have two males kennelled together. Good character and the absence of aggression, are of prime importance.

Chapter Ten

PRINCIPLES OF BREEDING

Before anybody ever has a litter from their Wirehair bitch, I hope that really serious consideration has been given to all the possible implications involved in such an action. You must know exactly the reasons why you are thinking of breeding puppies. If you have no real reason, then, to me, it is just a money-making motive.

THE PROS AND CONS

1. Do you really want to breed from your Wirehair bitch, to run the risk of serious veterinary problems? Most pregnancies and whelpings are without any complications whatsoever. However, occasionally it does happen that a bitch experiences problems which result in a caesarian section being done. Additionally it is not uncommon for a bitch, usually one who has had a large litter, to have an attack of eclampsia which could require an emergency visit from your vet to prevent her from dying. Consequently, before contemplating a litter, it is wise to have your bitch examined to ensure that she is fit enough to cope with pregnancy. This will also forewarn your vet of the impending pregnancy, should his services be needed.

2. A litter will do her good: Do not breed from your Wirehair bitch just because somebody has said that it will do her good. Having a litter will *not* save your Wirehair from the possibility of womb-related problems later in her life. Our vet has told us that the only way of being fairly sure of preventing womb problems and mammary problems is to have your bitch spayed before her first season. So, do not be fooled by that old wife's tale.

3. Have you got some prospective suitable homes ready and waiting for the subsequent puppies? You must remember that the Wirehair is still a relatively rare breed and so is rarely known by the general public. Consequently, correct, suitable homes are needed for the Wirehair and ideally these need to be found before your puppies arrive. If you have failed to do this for all of them, then you must advertise in the dog journals or the breed club information service when the puppies are about three weeks old.

4. Have you organised a way of having their tails docked? In most countries, the Wirehair still requires a docked tail to meet the breed requirements. It is also very necessary for any Wirehair destined to participate in the shooting field.

5. The average size of a litter: The size of the litter will be totally dependent on the number of eggs released by the bitch (ovulation) that are subsequently fertilised by the stud dog's sperm. The average size of a Wirehair litter is between eight and twelve puppies and, in exceptional cases, there have been litters of seventeen.

6. Time and cost factor: The time involved looking after your Wirehair before, during and after whelping is considerable. Remember that not all bitches are naturally good mothers. Combine this with the time taken up by interviews with prospective owners and weaning your puppies and it means that you will not have a tremendous amount left over.

The costs involved with the preparation of the whelping quarters, the extra feeding for both your bitch and her puppies, and any veterinary bills and advertising will all add up. Rarely does the sale of the puppies actually cover all the expenditure, especially if you have a small litter.

7. Do you realise the amount of work puppies cause when they are growing, before they are of an age to be sold? Most Wirehair bitches will start to become fed up with their puppies at about three to four weeks old. Consequently weaning will have to begin at this time. That means that, before long, you will be feeding all puppies individually four times a day, constantly cleaning their whelping quarters, administering a worming programme and starting to give basic socialisation training.

8. Have you got the room to provide adequate space for a litter? A suitable quiet place must be set aside for the whelping and rearing of the puppies. You might be able to provide the space somewhere in your home, but you might have to consider using an outside shed so that you will have more room available. This would be acceptable providing that the shed is clean and dry and you can provide the necessary heat and light for the puppies. Later on, the puppies will need an adequate and secure area, away from the sleeping quarters, to play in and to use for toilet purposes.

9. What happens if you are unable to sell the puppies at seven weeks old? You must consider that seven-week-old puppies still living in the nest will not be considered housetrained. Consequently, your workload will increase dramatically. Also remember that these growing puppies will become increasingly boisterous and will require more space in which to live until a buyer is found.

10. Your responsibility for puppies that you have bred: Do you realise, as the breeder of the puppies, you are responsible for all continuing welfare? Consequently, if one of your puppies was unfortunate enough to end up having to be taken in by the German Wirehaired Pointer Club Rescue, you would be asked to take back your Wirehair and assist with Rescue to find a new home, or at the very least provide financial support until a new home is found. Remember, it is the breeder who made the decision to bring puppies into the world.

If you feel that you cannot be sure of being able to answer all the questions positively, then why don't you consider purchasing another Wirehair puppy instead? This way you will not have the amount of hard work, combined with a lot of hassle, that is always associated with having a litter of Wirehair puppies.

THE MALE GERMAN WIREHAIRED POINTER

If your Wirehair is a male, then at some time you may consider allowing him to mate a bitch. Before you agree to this you must, once again, be fully aware of all the implications.

1. Are you sure that your Wirehair is of the correct type and temperament and is capable of

Am. Ch. Shurcan Baron of AfterHours, sire of thirty-two Champions, owned by Walt and Tina Whitmore. A stud dog must be of the correct type and temperament, and capable of passing on his virtues.

passing on virtues and not major faults?

2. Think about your own life style. Is your Wirehair a house dog? Have you any children, especially young ones? Does he live with other dogs, either male or female?

As soon as you allow any male dog to mate a bitch, you will transform your dog's character. It is inevitable that he will change and no longer be the dog that you knew. He will become more assertive in his manner towards both his family and surrounding dogs and, if this deviation remains unchecked, this character change may turn to aggression.

If you still wish your Wirehair to be used, then please be careful and do not allow him to mate a bitch until he is mature, at approximately two years of age. Choose a bitch that has been mated before and is accustomed to breeding, so, hopefully, his first experience will be relatively easy. A maiden bitch will be far from helpful and will fight against his advances, which is not a good idea.

After your Wirehair has successfully mated, give him time to adjust. Do not allow him to mate another bitch until you have had the opportunity to assess your Wirehair's character fully. The mating might not have changed him, but in most instances it will have. You might then realise that it is not such a good idea for your male to become a stud dog, and then be thankful that you only allowed him to mate one bitch.

One final point to remember. Any resulting litter is just as much your responsibility as it is for the bitch's owner.

THE BITCH

So, you have decided that you are going ahead with the idea of a litter. Well, hopefully, your bitch will be of the best bloodlines available to you and so be of excellent temperament and free from any major structural faults or unsoundness. To my mind, if there is any doubt

Sh. Ch. Bareve Barmelton. The brood bitch must be from the best bloodlines, of excellent temperament and free from any major structural faults.

John Hartley.

regarding her temperament, or her coat, then she should not be bred from. Do not think that your Wirehair bitch will produce excellent specimens if she herself has got faults. Remember that both her virtues and her faults will be passed on to the subsequent puppies – she will be contributing fifty per cent of the genes in her offspring.

No Wirehair bitch should be bred from until she has reached two years of age. As the Wirehair is slow maturing, it is necessary to give enough time for mental and physical growth before you embark on motherhood for her. Your bitch will first come into season at any time between six and eighteen months old. Obviously the actual age of the first season will depend on the overall maturity of your Wirehair. For instance, a very forward, well-grown bitch will probably come into season at about eight or nine months. However, it is quite common, with a very immature bitch, for her first season to occur when she is about fifteen to sixteen months. The time between seasons can vary considerably, ranging from four to nine months. Consequently, by the time your bitch is of an age to be bred from, she would have been in season at least twice, thereby establishing her own cycle.

If you intend to mate your Wirehair bitch on her next season and, due to her cycle, you know that this will happen soon, then it is vitally important to know when the first day of bleeding occurs.

We always put a white blanket into our Wirehair bitch's bed, so that we are instantly aware when there are any signs of a coloured discharge. Additionally we always "dab" our bitch's vulva with a white tissue, as this is another method of checking for colour. As soon as you first see any blood spots on either the blanket or the tissue, then that is considered the first day of her season. It is a good idea to actually wait until the next day to see if the bloody discharge does continue and, if so, then this is the time to contact the stud dog's owner and to set the date of the mating.

THE STUD DOG

Hopefully, you will have given plenty of time and thought to the possibility of stud dogs before your bitch actually comes into season. The eventual choice of stud dog should be the one you feel would best complement your bitch's quality and bloodlines and not just the latest Show Champion. You will need a Wirehair male whose construction and characteristics will give strength to your bitch's weakness and, in turn, your bitch's strengths will help to compensate for any weakness in the stud dog. At all times ensure that the combination of bloodlines is compatible and does not carry any hereditary problems. The attitude of those people who say "Any dog will do, because I am not prepared to travel", is completely wrong and proves that the breeding is not being done for the right reasons.

If you are in any doubt about the compatibility of any bloodlines, please contact an experienced breeder for advice before going ahead. It is much kinder to be "better safe than sorry" than to go ahead and risk having a litter of pups that will cause grief and sorrow. After all, in Germany, all breeding is monitored by Breedmeisters. These are people, chosen by the Breed Clubs, who have great knowledge of Wirehairs, bloodlines and the dog's individual capabilities. Consequently, no one is able to breed with their bitch until she has been "passed" by the region's Breedmeister with regard to her working ability, conformation and coat. You also cannot use a Stud dog that has not been passed by the Breedmeister.

Do remember that many of the recent Wirehairs are direct descendants of the three Dutch-bred imports and, because of the lack of new blood available at that time, there were many closely bred litters. We are more fortunate now because there are more bloodlines available, so it is no longer necessary, and certainly far from sensible, to mate very closely.

TYPES OF BREEDING

The three methods of breeding are linebreeding, inbreeding and outcrossing. Line breeding is breeding with a dog and bitch that are originally from the same bloodlines but with a percentage of unrelated dogs and bitches in each side of the pedigree. This is a good method of doubling up with the type that you prefer by using the good characteristics, but you must remember the unrelated dogs might carry a trait that you would rather do without. However, I would consider that this is the best option to try if you wish to continue with the type and characteristics you started with.

Beware of breeding too close. This is called inbreeding. This is where you are breeding with a dog and bitch that are so closely related that they are probably father to daughter, mother to son, brother to sister or even half-brother to half-sister. This close relationship can be a possible minefield due to the fact that you will be doubling up on *every* characteristic of the dog and bitch. This might not be considered too bad regarding all the good points of the dog and bitch in question, but what about the faults? Do not forget that you would be getting two helpings of those as well. *This method should be left to the experienced breeders who are only too aware of the risks and implications.*

Outcrossing is where you breed a dog and bitch with only a few, or no, shared ancestors. Your puppies will then have a complete mixture of both the dog's and the bitch's characteristics. However, it will also mean that your subsequent litter will be of different types, thereby defeating the object in trying to improve the breed by producing similar types.

If you are a novice, then I feel it is better to use an experienced stud dog who has already proved that he is capable of producing typy puppies. The problem with using a Wirehair dog for the first time is that you will not have had the opportunity to see what he can produce. I know that the resulting quality of the puppies is not totally dependent on the stud dog in question. Nevertheless, if you have only got one Wirehair bitch and you feel that you only want this one litter, then it is a better idea to use a Wirehair dog that has produced typy puppies – rather than using the unknown and producing a litter that is not really what you wanted.

Do not forget, when breeding, that each parent will be passing on the genes obtained from parents and grandparents and all antecedents. Occasionally you will have an exceptional Wirehair born from either a mediocre parent or parents, and it is this factor that you should bear in mind when using a stud dog. It is just not the quality of the Wirehair dog in question: it is the quality of the Wirehairs behind both the stud dog and your own bitch.

MAKING THE ARRANGEMENTS

When you have made your decision as to which stud dog you would like to use, it is good manners to ask the owners, well in advance of your bitch coming into season, for consent to allow the dog to mate your bitch. Not every Wirehair dog you see will be at stud, because some live with children, some with other males, some with both, and consequently they are not considered to be stud dogs. Do not rant and rave if the owners refuse permission. Just be sensible and respect their wishes. After all, it is their dog and they are the people who live with him.

If the owner agrees to allow the dog to mate your bitch, you need to investigate the terms involved. You must find out what the stud fee will be. This is quite a personal thing, but you must be prepared to pay at least the cost of a puppy. Sometimes the stud dog owner will consider having a puppy in lieu of a stud fee. If this is the case, it will certainly ease the problem of finding one suitable home, but please establish at this point whether it will be the first or second pick of litter. It can be very disheartening to overlook this fact and then have the stud dog owner come in, take first pick of the litter and choose the puppy you had decided to keep for yourself.

The stud fee is due to be paid at the time of the successful mating unless a puppy is being given to the owner in lieu. Do not forget to find out what will happen if your bitch fails to conceive or fails to have a live litter. In normal circumstances, in either of these two events, a free return mating is offered. However, the conditions are what the stud dog's owner makes them, and you have to abide by them. The stud fee is a payment for the actual mating and not necessarily for the resulting puppies. If your bitch fails to conceive and you have used a stud dog who has proved capable of producing puppies, then you must consider that the fault will almost certainly lie with your bitch. This does not mean that your bitch is infertile. It could be that you took her for mating on the wrong day, either too early or too late.

However, if she misses a second time to the same dog who is still producing puppies, then you must understand that you have probably got a fertility problem, which will require veterinary attention. Subsequent visits to the same stud dog will, more than likely, have to be accompanied by the payment of another stud fee.

Some owners of stud dogs insist that your bitch goes to your vet for a vaginal swab to be taken to ensure that she is free from infection. Should the vet find that she has a low-grade infection, a simple course of antibiotics, taken a few days before mating, will ensure that no infection is either transmitted to the stud dog, or will prevent the bitch conceiving.

THE MATING

Your Wirehair bitch is in season and by the second day you have contacted the owner of the stud dog to find out when to take her. We mate our Wirehair bitches on the eleventh and thirteenth days, but you would really have to be guided by the reaction of the stud dog. It is normal practice for the bitch to visit the stud dog. From the start of her season until the visit to the stud dog, your bitch must be kept well away from other males to prevent an accident from occurring.

On arrival, the bitch will be introduced to the stud dog, whilst still on her lead, in the allotted area set aside for the mating to take place. Her initial reaction will nearly always be very uncooperative. I feel that, for the first few moments, she should be restricted to some degree so that she is not in a position to bite the keen stud dog and cause him to become unsure. Do not be too surprised if the stud dog owner asks you to leave your bitch with them until the mating has been accomplished. It is quite surprising how many bitches are uncooperative while their owner is still around and become much more responsive once the owner is out of sight. If you are asked to do this then do not worry, because, as soon as the dog has achieved the mating, you will be called to witness that the job has been done.

Once the bitch's natural uneasy attitude wears off and she starts to relax we allow her more freedom so she can flirt and encourage the dog to mount her. At this point we take hold of the bitch's collar to ensure that she does not bite and injure him or move away at the crucial time. While the bitch is 'standing' and encouraging the dog to mount her, she will instinctively hold her tail to one side to assist penetration. As he climbs on to her back he will use his front legs to hold himself in position whilst he searches for her swollen vulva. If the stud dog is experienced, and your bitch is receptive, he should not have too much trouble penetrating her.

On penetration he will start to ejaculate and swell. It is this swelling, coupled with the muscular constriction of the bitch's vagina, that causes the dogs to be "tied". After a few moments of being tied, the stud dog will instinctively remove his front legs from around the bitch and attempt to lift one hind leg over the bitch's back. In most cases this 'turning' will be supervised by the stud dog's owner to prevent any injury occurring to either the dog or the bitch.

This final position, with the dog and bitch literally being back to back, can last from ten minutes to approximately forty-five minutes. At this point, the visiting bitch's owner will be invited to return, to witness that the mating has been successful and to hold the bitch to prevent her from fidgeting. The length of the tie is totally dependent on the bitch, because she is holding the dog with this contraction of her vagina. Once the contraction relaxes, the bitch releases the dog and they naturally come away from each other. At no time during the mating should they be forced apart, as this could lead to serious internal injuries to both dog and bitch.

If your bitch is too early or too late she will probably not become receptive in any way and should not be forced into being mated. If she is too early but flirts excessively to the point of being mated, she may not be able to constrict her vagina sufficiently to hold the dog and he may 'slip' her. This is quite common with an early bitch and, if that should happen, you will need to remove her from the stud dog, who should be taken away so that he can sort himself out and return his penis back within its sheath.

Some stud dogs never really tie, but they can ejaculate enough semen inside the bitch for her to conceive; so if this happens to your bitch do not assume that, because they did not tie, she will not produce any puppies. It is not ideal, but, as it is not impossible, you will have to wait and see. On arrival home, you will still have to ensure that your bitch is kept isolated, as it is still possible for her to be mated by another dog.

THE PREGNANCY

The actual gestation period is sixty three days, but it is more likely that a bitch, especially one whelping for the first time, will give birth three to four days earlier. Occasionally bitches may go over the time, but that normally occurs if the bitch has only a few puppies, rather than a normal-size litter. In the first four weeks after mating, there should be no change to your bitch's lifestyle at all. She should be allowed to exercise as normal and she certainly should not have any increase of food.

Then you should start to notice the obvious signs which indicate that she is in whelp. She will probably start to look after herself more and her nipples, especially those first ones found right behind her elbow, will become pink and erect. If you wish to have her scanned to make sure that she is pregnant, then this is the time when vets prefer to do it. At this stage they can see clearly the number of puppies in the uterus, but in the later stages it is not so easy to determine how many there are.

At about five weeks you should be able to see a definite thickening around your bitch's middle. At this point you should start to increase her food gradually. Take care not to overfeed at any stage, as a fat bitch is never an easy whelper. If you are providing a good-quality food, there is little point in also giving a lot of additives, as you could be doing more harm than good. If you are in any doubt, then contact your vet who will advise you accordingly. As you increase her food, do not change the amounts dramatically: it is far more sensible to increase the number of feeds rather than the amount at each meal time. She will probably become very reluctant to exercise as she increases in size. However, your bitch will need to be fit to ensure that the whelping is as trouble-free as possible. Consequently, you may have to take her for short walks daily, but do restrict her from playing roughly or with other dogs.

You should, at this point, already have in hand where she is going to whelp. Her whelping box should be large enough so that she can lie down flat and should give her enough room so that she is not forced to lie immediately below the heat lamp which you will have to use for the new-born pups. Three of the sides should be of sufficient height to stop draughts.

The front of the box should be constructed so that it can be totally removed during whelping, to enable you to assist if necessary. After whelping it needs to be either removed, or reduced in height, so that your bitch can safely enter the whelping box after relieving herself without any danger of stepping on her puppies.

Another necessity for the whelping box is an inner safety rail. This needs to be attached at approximately six inches from the floor and to be approximately six inches wide. When this rail is fixed it means that, if the bitch lies down with the puppies behind her, they will be pushed into the space below it and avoid being either crushed by her body or squashed against the side of the whelping box.

Wherever you decide your bitch is going to whelp, you must ensure that there is a constant temperature of not less than 68 degrees and not more than 72 degrees Fahrenheit. If you cannot be sure of regulating the temperature accordingly, then it may be necessary to use a heat-and-light bulb. We used to use infra-red lamps for this purpose but we now find it very difficult to obtain them, so we use either 150 or 200 watt heat-and-light bulbs, depending on the weather, which ensure that there is a constant heat over the new-born puppies. If it is cold weather, then do take care not to have the lamp hanging too low. Not only will you run the risk of over-heating the puppies, but you will certainly make your bitch uncomfortably hot. She will then lie away from the heat and from her puppies, thereby depriving them of her care.

The floor of the whelping box should be covered with newspapers. As soon as your bitch shows signs of being in whelp, then is the time to start collecting newspapers. It is surprising how much you will use, so it is better to start with the largest pile you can manage to collect.

You will need to introduce your bitch to her whelping quarters well in advance. We begin to introduce our bitches when they have about a week left to go before the due date, as this enables the bitch to become settled before she whelps. Obviously, until she actually starts to whelp, you can still use your bitch's own blanket in the box, as that will encourage her to settle in her new surroundings.

The last item you will need to include in the whelping quarters is a radio. The constant playing of a radio will override all the noises that occur outside the whelping quarters. Your bitch will not be able to hear anything she might interpret as a threat to her puppies, or all the normal family sounds, which might make her want to leave her puppies and rejoin the familiar way of life. Additionally, when the puppies are of an age to be able to take in what is happening around them, they will by then be used to hearing all the sounds associated with the radio.

Chapter Eleven

WHELPING AND REARING

THE WHELPING

As the due time draws near, your Wirehair will start to display the classic signs associated with whelping. She will become very restless, start to tear up her newspapers and endeavour to dig in order to make her own bed. Remove her own blanket and make sure that there are sufficient layers of newspaper laid down, so that as each puppy is born only the top layers of paper will need to be removed and replaced.

It is most likely that she will refuse her food and this will normally correspond with constant visits outside in an attempt to 'empty herself out' so that, when she is ready to whelp, she will not be desperate to leave her puppies in order to relieve herself. Her temperature will start to drop, and she will begin to shiver, yet she will also start panting and maybe also whine. One of the last pre-whelping signs will be the 'breaking of the waters' and this may happen whilst she is outside relieving herself, or inside in her whelping box as she starts the first, minor contractions. All these normal signs may go on for several hours before she actually has her first puppy.

As the first puppy is pushed into the birth canal this will stimulate the bitch to begin straining in an effort to push the puppy out. Upon arrival you will see that, normally, the puppy is enclosed in a fluid-filled sac which should immediately open itself. If the sac does not rupture or the bitch fails to open it, then you must tear it open yourself. The puppy in the birth canal is not breathing independently but, as soon as the birth occurs, then breathing will automatically begin. If the puppy is still encased in the sac when this happens, the surrounding fluid will be inhaled, instead of air. Consequently, it is essential that, as soon as the puppy is born, the sac is removed so that the puppy breathes air rather than fluid. A puppy remaining in the sac will certainly die from drowning.

If you feel that the new-born puppy is not breathing very well then take a soft towel and rub the puppy's back and sides briskly. This should give sufficient stimulation to encourage steady breathing. Make sure that the mouth and nostrils are clear of any mucus and fluid which might also impair breathing.

Your bitch will, at this stage, attempt to remove the placenta and she will be vigorously licking at her puppy. Normally she will break the umbilical cord herself, but do take care that she does not sever it too close to the puppy. We actually insist that we cut the cord ourselves, with a pair of sterilized scissors, rather than allowing the bitch to do it. With one hand pinching the cord at about two inches from the puppy, we use the pair of scissors to 'chew' through the cord, taking small snips, rather than cutting the cord with one big movement. Should your bitch remove the cord too closely to the puppy or should the cord start to bleed, then you will have to tie a piece of sterilised cotton tightly around it which stops the bleeding.

If your bitch wants to clear up and eat the placenta, then that is fine, but we normally restrict the number. We allow the bitch the first one and then we insist that she allows us to remove the placenta, along with the soiled paper, after each subsequent puppy is born. Once the puppy has been cleaned and is breathing steadily then place the puppy next to the bitch to start searching for the nipples. You must try and encourage the puppy to suckle as soon as possible as this stimulates the bitch and helps with the subsequent contractions and strainings.

Have a cardboard box, with a hot-water bottle wrapped in a towel sitting in it, ready for the next arrival. As soon as your bitch starts to strain and to lick her vulva in readiness for the next puppy, her attention will be taken up with the forthcoming birth and she could accidentally hurt any puppies that are actually with her. So, at this point, we normally remove the new-born puppy and place it in the cardboard box for safety, whilst the next puppy is being born. During whelping, we only allow one puppy to be with its mother at any time, as we consider that she has enough to occupy her mind and that the puppies are safer and are warm in the cardboard box.

Puppies will be born at varying intervals. Initially the puppies may be born quite quickly, but as the whelping continues, then the time between the puppies will probably increase. In a normal whelping your bitch will only need to give a few intense 'pushes' and the puppy will be born. If she is producing frequent shallow pushes and is getting very tired and distressed and achieving nothing, then you must call in the vet, especially if this has been happening for more that a hour. You must also call the vet if the fluids, which are discharged and are normally dark green in colour, change to black. This in an indication of foetal distress.

A delay may mean that a puppy is going to be born in the breech position. If this is so, then you must watch carefully and be ready to assist if necessary. As the puppy presents itself, tail first, be prepared with a towel and, as soon as you can, hold on, to prevent the puppy slipping back into the bitch as her contraction subsides. As soon as she starts to strain again, you can help her by maintaining the pressure, without actually pulling on the puppy, until it is safely away. Immediately, check the mouth and nostrils and, in most cases, you will have to use the towel and stimulate breathing.

In other cases it could mean that there is not a puppy presenting, or that the puppy presenting may be dead. Your bitch may need an injection to enable her to push the puppy along and eventually give birth. If, after an injection, she is still experiencing problems, then your vet will probably insist that a caesarean section is performed, as it is likely that one of the puppies has caused an obstruction. If this is the case, then your vet will be able to give you advice regarding the after-care of your bitch and her resulting puppies.

Assuming that the whelping has progressed without experiencing any problems, your bitch will start to relax immediately she has finished. As soon as it is possible, ask your vet to visit and check both your bitch and her puppies. Your vet will probably administer an injection to your bitch, as this will help clear her uterus of any retained placentas, will help her to relax and will boost her milk supply.

Once you are sure that she has finally finished, your bitch and her puppies should be left in peace and quiet to recuperate. It is a good idea to offer her a drink and, if you have restrained her from clearing up all the placentas, then you could offer her a small meal. Within hours of finishing we always ensure that the whelping quarters are made clean with a plentiful supply of newspaper laid down. On top of these we always 'tack' down either a piece of carpet or some dog bedding. This is needed to ensure that the puppies will have a non-slip surface on which to get a purchase when they are trying to keep in contact with their mother. It also helps to maintain a cosier, warmer surface than can be achieved with newspaper.

You should restrict any family visits until after the mother has rested sufficiently. It is not a good idea to invite strangers to visit your bitch and her new-born puppies. We never allow anyone unknown to visit ours until the puppies are approximately five weeks old. There are too many risks associated with visitors. Not only do you run the danger of passing on infections, you will also risk upsetting your bitch and she may end up either becoming over-protective, or rejecting her litter and leaving you with a hand-rearing operation.

NEW-BORN PUPPIES
New-born puppies spend most of their early days sleeping and feeding, and contented, warm and well-fed puppies are always quiet. If your puppies are making a considerable amount of noise then they are probably either hungry or cold. Make sure that the whelping quarters are warm enough and if you are happy with that, then check your bitch's milk supply. While she is rearing her puppies she will require additional food, and unlimited access to liquids, to enable her to produce sufficient milk. If you feel that you are feeding her adequately and yet her milk is either not very plentiful or of a green colour, then contact your vet, as she will require some treatment.

New-born puppies, when handled, give the impression of being firm and rounded, but sickly puppies always go limp. Consequently, we pick up each puppy at least once daily to ascertain that the puppy is thriving and is not in need of treatment. If you have a sickly puppy then your bitch will instinctively know and will constantly be seen to 'push it out', demonstrating nature's way of only rearing the strongest.

Docking will need to be done after three or four days. If you have found someone suitable to dock your puppies, then it is best if they visit you, rather than you having to transport your bitch and her litter to their premises. As I have said previously, docking is essential and it is not done for cosmetic reasons. We do not remove dewclaws, as we feel that they do not cause great problems, provided they are kept short in adult life.

When your puppies are about ten to twelve days old the eyelids will begin to open but sight will still be undeveloped. If any of the puppies' eyes are not open by about fifteen days, then do not delay but contact your vet, as there will be a reason for this and it will need veterinary treatment if there is a minor infection. At two weeks the puppies' nails should be clipped, to prevent them from scratching and damaging your bitch's teats. This should be repeated as often as necessary.

Between three and four weeks of age the puppies will start to become quite active. The senses of smell, sight and hearing begin to develop more fully so that, by five weeks, the puppies' movements are co-ordinated and there is an awareness of sounds and other activities and a readiness to start learning about life.

WEANING

At three weeks of age you should be starting to wean the puppies. We start our puppies off using a substitute milk product twice a day. Each puppy is individually introduced to it on a saucer. For our convenience and ease, we always stand each puppy up on a work-surface on a towel so that posture can be maintained and there is no slipping. Hold the puppy with the flat of your hand underneath the rib cage, with your fingers lifting and holding the forequarters. You are then fully supporting the puppy and giving a feeling of confidence. Most puppies will have been used to lifting their heads to feed from the bitch, but now you have got to teach them to lower their heads and feed from a saucer. Feeding puppies individually gives you the chance to devote more time to each puppy whilst you are persuading them to feed in this way.

Initial feeding sessions are very traumatic to the puppies. Not only do they end up with more food on them than inside them, but it really does cause the puppies to become shocked. As soon as they have all been fed, we always return the bitch to them, as this encourages the puppies to suckle from her and then to settle and sleep off the exertion.

Once the puppies have become efficient at taking the milk product from a saucer, we introduce a pre-soaked complete puppy food. At least one hour before we feed the puppies, we soak a quantity of this, using pre-boiled water. When it has expanded, increased and softened in texture, we mash it down to a size that the puppies will be able to cope with and we remove any bits that have failed to soften and would require chewing. We then feed the puppies in the same individual way. At this stage, the puppies will still be licking at their food, which is why we mash it down so that they can eat it this way.

We do not like to use scraped or chopped meat as an introductory food, for the simple fact that it may be very difficult to guarantee the freshness other than by buying expensive trays of meat from butchers. When you first start to wean puppies, the last thing you want is to encourage stomach upsets, which do happen with meat that is less than fresh. There is no doubt that puppies enjoy the smell and taste of chopped meat, but unless you can afford to pay for good quality, it is far easier to rear puppies on a tried and tested complete puppy food.

By the time the puppies are four weeks old and are readily eating off the saucer, we introduce another two meals, so that they are being fed four times a day. Feeding them individually would be very time-consuming, so at this point we start to feed them together in the whelping quarters, but we ensure that each puppy actually feeds from a separate dish. This also stops any puppy pushing the smaller ones away from the food and guards against any puppy over-eating.

Being fed four meals of the same substance daily may seem very repetitious, but the puppies do not think that way and will readily eat this food until they are about four months

ABOVE: A nice, evenly-matched litter. The puppies are now weaned and independent of their mother.

RIGHT: Two seven-week-old litter brothers, showing different amounts of facial whiskers.

old before they show signs of boredom. Keeping the puppies on the same diet during weaning, worming, homing and completion of the vaccination programme will give them an ideal start in life. After this time, you can introduce any method of feeding, providing it is done gradually.

After each meal, a dish of water should be introduced to the litter. Puppies need liquid in addition to their food. They must be able to manage the intake of water, coupled with eating solid foods. Do not make their solid food too mushy; it is far better to feed the food slightly dry and offer water afterwards. Initially it is not a good idea to leave a dish of water with them, as they will probably play in it or tip it up, leaving their bed very wet. However, by about five to six weeks of age, a dish of water, firmly and safely fixed, should be left with the litter. If the puppies are still fascinated by the water and are standing over the dish drinking solidly, reduce the amount of water in the dish and only increase this when it is no longer a novelty to them.

Also, at four weeks, once the puppies are eating well, we begin the worming and vaccination programme. All of our puppies are given a parvo vaccination as a precautionary measure. If the puppies' natural immunity is still quite high at this age, the injection will basically be a waste of money and time, as that immunity will counteract the serum. However, it usually starts to wane at this stage, so more often than not, the injection will top the puppies up and give them more protection.

Do not worm your puppies at the same time, as it will cause unnecessary upset. Make sure that at least three days elapse before you commence worming. Ask your vet to supply you with sufficient worming tablets for the whole of the litter and follow all advice fully. Do not over-dose, and certainly do not buy any form of worming preparation from pet shops or stores.

Between four and five weeks of age you can start to keep the bitch away from her puppies more than once during the day and throughout the night. Certainly, when you worm the puppies, it is good idea to keep the bitch away for a while, so that she is unable to clear up after the puppies whilst they are passing worms. She might have already shown signs of being sick and tired of them by this time, but in any event the puppies must start to get used to being on their own.

Some very good mothers will begin regurgitating their food for the puppies, so it is advisable to keep the bitch away from the litter for a while after she has been fed. It may well be nature's way of providing for the puppies once they have stopped suckling. We personally prefer them not to have access to this food. It will be different from the food that you are using to wean them, and the puppies will not be too keen to feed from a dish at their next meal. By the time the puppies are five weeks old they should be pretty well weaned away from their mother. She will probably be showing signs of being sick of them and their demanding ways, and will be looking for the chance to return to her normal way of life. It is likely that she will still want to check on her puppies but will not want to spend any amount of time with them, visibly preferring the release from motherhood.

When the puppies have reached six weeks of age they have their first complete vaccination, combined with a vetting. This ensures that your puppies are given a clean bill of health before they are sold. It also gives both yourself and the puppies a least a week before they are due to go to their new homes. This way they will have time to recover from any possible reaction to the vaccines. At seven weeks your puppies should be prepared and ready to go to their new families. Ensure that each puppy is readily eating four meals a day and that the new owners are given a diet sheet, together with at least a week's supply of food, so that there is no reason to change the diet and risk an upset tummy.

Chapter Twelve

THE WORKING WIREHAIR

TRAINING THE WIREHAIR

As in any form of training, a bond must be formed between handler and dog. This process should begin immediately you buy your puppy. If your require your Wirehair for working, then it is far easier teaching a puppy your requirements, than a partially-grown Wirehair with pre-set training. I feel that it is essential to do the training yourself, rather than sending your Wirehair away to a professional trainer. Trainers with experience of HPRs are not as numerous as those for Spaniels and Retrievers.

You will need access to a piece of land, a regular period of time set aside each day, a long training lead or rope, a couple of dummies and two whistles, one of a certain pitch, for example 210 or 210.5, and the other a referee's whistle. Most of the early lessons can be done in your home and garden.

The main problem with training is the fact that your Wirehair is not a mind-reader. Ideally, you must teach your Wirehair to do things the right way before any bad habits creep in. In order to obey commands, your Wirehair must know and understand what is being asked. For example, on the command of Sit, your Wirehair must initially be made to sit and eventually be obedient to this command. Do not confuse things by using different commands or long sentences, sometimes "Sit", sometimes "Sit down", and at other times "Get down". Always be consistent, use the same commands, together with the same tone of voice.

From the beginning you must bear in mind the need for obedience. Once a command has been clearly given, you must ensure that you are obeyed first time. This aspect should never be overlooked under any circumstances. It is extremely important, at any stage of training. If it is not stressed during the early stages of training, it will become increasingly hard to overcome later when disobedience will have become a habit.

However, remember that individual dogs develop at different rates. The exact age at which to start intensive training will depend on your own Wirehair's temperament and characteristics. Most Wirehair puppies are able to start intensive training at about six months of age. You can use the initial few months teaching the real basic commands of Come, No, Sit, Down, Heel and, most important, your Wirehair's name. Always ensure that the early lessons are short and are associated with fun and praise where appropriate. Never be boring or tedious. Provided you follow these straight forward suggestions, your Wirehair puppy will look forward to lessons with you, thereby creating that essential bonding relationship.

Pola del Chisola, Aloysia Hard's third Italian import. Wirehairs learn at different rates, and you must be sensitive to your dog's mental development.

Always observe your puppy and try to be one jump ahead, to enable you to anticipate any reactions. It is essential to avoid any sign of your puppy becoming bored. If you are under the impression that this is happening, or that by insisting on finishing a particular exercise you will cause your puppy to fail to complete it successfully, then stop. Immediately set an easier exercise that will be readily obeyed, thus enabling you always to end training sessions on a successful note.

Punishment should, ideally, never feature in training. If you do ever feel that a line of punishment is needed, then it is vitally important to connect it with the offence. If you cannot administer it immediately, then it is best avoided. For example, it is not beneficial to punish a dog who moves during a stay, when what you should have done was prevent the movement in the first place, even if it meant issuing another command. Never, ever lose either your temper or your patience; remember that your Wirehair is not a mind-reader and that any mistake, or failure to obey, is most probably caused by your vague instructions.

FIRST LESSONS

As I said previously, most of the early lessons can be done in your garden. It is far from sensible to start lessons in an area so large that you are unable to keep control and remain in charge. You, as the handler, need to set the required standards and, to do so, you must adopt the dominant position. Never, at any stage, allow your puppy to challenge your decisions.

Apart from your Wirehair's name, the first essential command is No. This is a general term which your puppy will soon realise means disapproval and stopping the current activity. It should not be over-used in the early days and should only be given when you are able to reinforce it.

To teach your puppy to Sit and Stay, early lessons include using these commands before feeding. This technique teaches your puppy to obey a command which is then rewarded with food. As time progresses, you can increase the length of stays from seconds to minutes. You can continue this exercise in your garden, both at feed time and when other opportunities present themselves. The extra room will enable you to lengthen the distance between yourself and your puppy.

INTRODUCTION TO THE WHISTLES

During these early lessons you need to introduce the whistles. Right from the start you need to decide which system of whistle commands to use to convey messages. I use one toot to stop, two toots for a change of direction, and three toots for recall. Throughout training, I always use one toot on the referee's whistle as the command to stop. The other commands are given on the other whistle.

When you start to teach your puppy to come back to you, use a combination of voice and whistle. During play in the garden, call your puppy's name, give three toots and call the name again. Keep repeating these commands until the puppy returns. If your puppy seems reluctant to return, then walk away, still giving the commands, and it is very unlikely that your puppy will fail to follow you. On returning, give great praise and cast the puppy free again. Never restrict your puppy immediately, because then returning will be connected with loss of freedom and there will be a subsequent reluctance to obey. In a short time your Wirehair will return on the whistle command alone, and then you can stop using the name.

Heel work is essential and can be started as soon as your puppy readily accepts the lead. You do not need to teach fancy commands like Reverse About Turn and others, but your puppy does need to learn to sit as soon as you stop. First lessons will involve you physically placing your puppy in the sitting position, using a combination of voice, raised hand and a stamped foot. As soon as your Wirehair will sit, untouched, at the moment you stop, you can then introduce the whistle. Command your Wirehair to sit and then immediately give a blast on the stop whistle. This exercise is usually learnt quickly on the lead and in no time at all your Wirehair will sit on just the whistle.

Unfortunately, once you progress to doing exercises off the lead, your Wirehair may start to try it on. During a training session, when your Wirehair puppy is loose in the garden, give a blast on the stop whistle for the command "Sit". If this is not obeyed, you must sprint across to where your puppy is and enforce it. Return your puppy to the exact spot where the initial command was received. Give the whistle command again and make the puppy sit. Do not allow any movement away from the original place. Make sure that the exercise is completed in the original position.

In the early stages of teaching your Wirehair puppy to drop to the whistle, do not call from the sitting position. If you do, it will encourage your Wirehair to anticipate your commands and be too ready and eager to move. It is advisable always to go to the puppy, as this enforces the steadiness that is associated with a stay exercise. If, at any time, your Wirehair refuses to stay put on this command, or continues to move, then you must go back to the basic heel work and reinforce the commands. It is vitally important that your Wirehair will stop on command, because, when you are with game, even the most obedient dog may become slightly deaf. If there are any flaws at this stage, then it is a certainty that you will be in deep trouble when you get amongst the real thing.

RETRIEVING

The instinct to pick things up should be encouraged right from the start. Most cases of Wirehairs not being good retrievers have been caused by the owners. More often than not a puppy will be carrying something that is not allowed. Instead of remonstrating with yourself for being careless in leaving the object around in the first place and carefully removing the

Can. Ch. Hennum's Duchess Wilhelm enthusiastically entering water for a retrieve.

Am. Ch. Spindrifters Mark of Laurwyns swimming with a dummy. The Wirehair's coat is ideally suited to working in water.

retrieve, you will probably snatch it from your puppy's mouth and show that you are cross. No wonder, then, that the puppy becomes hesitant about retrieving, if it always results in a scolding. Additionally, never get involved in a tug-of-war, as this may result in your Wirehair developing a hard mouth. So, remember, each time a treasured retrieve is being shown off, to call your puppy to you by name, give lots of praise and carefully remove the object in conjunction with the command "Dead".

When you start the proper retrieving lessons, use an object that your puppy has already taken a fancy to, such as an old shoe or a play toy. As soon as your Wirehair readily picks up an object, introduce a small light weight dummy. Rather than buy a ready-made puppy dummy, use an old sock stuffed tightly with old rags or material. As your puppy grows you can then introduce the normal-sized dummy. You need a clean pick-up, so do not introduce too heavy a dummy, as it may cause your puppy difficulty in retrieving properly to hand.

Am. Ch. Ali del Chisola executing a confident retrieve.

Game must be retrieved tenderly to hand.

Only the early retrieves are done with the dummy thrown in full view. If your Wirehair attempts to run after it, that is acceptable. Steadiness can come later. Such treasure will usually be taken straight to the puppy's basket, so bear that in mind when you plan the exercise. Place yourself in a direct line with the route to the basket and throw the dummy approximately six feet away, giving the command "Fetch". Allow your puppy to follow straightaway and pick up the dummy. Then, as the puppy runs back to the basket, intercept and gently remove the dummy with the command "Dead" and, as always, praise. The next stage is gentle restraint while the dummy is thrown, allowing the puppy to go only when the dummy lands. Eventually you reach the stage of making the puppy Sit and Stay until commanded to Go and Retrieve.

As soon as your Wirehair knows that, on the command of Fetch, there is an object to be retrieved, you can then introduce retrieves when the dummy is not in sight. You must not allow your puppy to depend on eyesight for retrieves. You must encourage the use of the nose. After commanding your Wirehair to Sit, throw the dummy into a clump of long grass. After the initial steadiness, give the command "Fetch" and release your Wirehair. Your puppy will start to sniff around trying to locate the dummy by scent. When you think that your puppy is in the right area, give the command "Hi lost". As soon as your Wirehair locates the dummy and retrieves it, give great praise. If you keep using this command when you consider that your puppy is in the right area, the connection will soon be made.

HUNTING

Once your Wirehair puppy has a reasonable knowledge of the basic commands, you can introduce training for hunting and quartering ground. The eventual hunting range of your Wirehair will depend upon character, coupled with training and experience.

Right from the start, it is essential for you to check the direction of the wind and ensure that you work your Wirehair into the wind. Position yourself in the centre of the piece of land you intend your Wirehair to hunt and give the command "Sit". It is advisable to use a field rather than walking up tracks or along hedgerows, because a field allows freedom to range, whereas tracks and hedges encourage work in straight lines in front of you, rather than natural quartering.

After the initial short sit, tell your Wirehair to "Get on" or "Seek on" and go off either to the left or right of you. Encourage this forward movement by using hand signals, coupled with the command. In the early stages, the actual direction of hunting is not as important as keeping your Wirehair in front of you and not allowing any quartering of the ground behind you. Assuming that your Wirehair will come back when called, then you can allow quite free ranging. It is far easier to bring a dog in closer to within a reasonable distance than it is to push one out to increase the range.

As your Wirehair starts to work to your left, you must turn and begin walking to your right without your dog seeing you change direction. Once your change of direction has been noticed, your Wirehair will turn and start to work towards you. As soon as your Wirehair crosses in front of you and continues to work, turn in the other direction and keep repeating these changes. This is the basis of quartering. This exercise also encourages your Wirehair

A spectacular picture of Severn Run's Flying Finish being steady to the flush of quail during a training session with owner Elizabeth Barrett.

to keep looking to see where you are. However, please remember that quartering involves covering a lot of ground. Whilst you are only walking a short distance, your Wirehair is covering a lot more ground, working from side to side. Keep the exercises short and never let your Wirehair get to the plodding stage because of tiredness.

Once your Wirehair is successfully quartering into the wind and is changing direction in line with you, the whistle commands can be introduced. Allow your dog to quarter away from you, then change direction and, on doing so, give two toots on the whistle. This should produce an immediate response, so when your dog, on hearing the whistle, looks towards you, use your out-stretched arm to indicate a change of direction. I feel it is easier to use two toots for a change of direction, rather than two distinct whistle commands for left and right.

POINTING

Pointing is a natural instinct for the Wirehair, so it is best to encourage any show of it from an early age, rather than ignore these promising signs. A number of people use a rabbit pen to teach the Wirehair to point. Consequently, it is advisable to use a lead. As soon as your Wirehair scents the rabbit, he will probably stop without warning and freeze. On seeing this pose, you should approach slowly and stroke your dog while giving the command "Steady". If you approach quickly and make a noise, you may cause your Wirehair to break the point by looking round at you, or by running in.

Once your Wirehair is on point you should count to ten before you continue with the next stage. This encourages the Wirehair to remain steady. When you are happy with the length of time that the point has been held, you must then flush the rabbit yourself and ensure that your Wirehair drops to the flush. Even if the rabbit breaks the eye contact and runs, you should still make your Wirehair drop to the flush. You must insist on this, because in the long term it helps prevent any running in or chasing of game.

Am. Ch. Cadenberg Gernot V Lutz, owned by Joseph and Sara Langlois, holding a successful point.

*Am. Ch.
Flintocks
Medicine Man
pointing
pheasant in
Montana.*

*Dual Ch.
Cascade Rogue
and Field
Ch./Am. Field
Ch. Cascade
Steamer,
pointing and
backing.*

As soon as your Wirehair has become relatively staunch at pointing, you can dispense with the lead. You may also wish to try different types of game, other than rabbits in a pen. Working into the wind will assist in finding suitable game to point. The first sign of your Wirehair being successful will be a distinctive wagging tail carriage. At this stage you should be watching carefully and, if necessary, be prepared to blow the stop whistle if the point is not held and the game is flushed too quickly. If your Wirehair points staunchly at something, then try to get there as speedily and as quietly as possible. If you manage to achieve this, count to ten, flush the game yourself and enforce the dropped position. Unfortunately, in attempting to get to your Wirehair's side, you may flush the game prematurely. If this happens, be ready with the stop whistle to prevent any chasing.

Providing that the command to the flush will be obeyed, you can continue to put your Wirehair amongst game in an attempt to perfect the pointing ability. You cannot expect perfect, classic points every time. Some days your Wirehair will freeze and give clear indication that there is game but will actually keep all four feet on the ground. Whatever position your Wirehair adopts for pointing, it is by far one of the most spectacular aspects of a working gundog.

Chapter Thirteen

SPECIALISED ACTIVITIES

DEER STALKING

If your interests are in deer stalking, you will have purchased your Wirehair with this specialised activity in mind. Time-consuming training will be required to teach the skills necessary for tracking killed and wounded deer.

You will need obedience at all times, because your dog must always walk quietly at heel and go down and stay on command, while you disappear out of sight. It is essential for your dog to be quiet at all times and be capable of being patient whilst awaiting your commands. This is a sport where things do not happen quickly, so a dog that whines and is always bouncing around waiting to go, is far from ideal. The Wirehair is a breed noted for quietness whilst waiting and therefore quite a popular choice for the professional deer stalker. Before you can start the specialist training, your Wirehair will need to be trained to the basic level required of any gundog.

METHODS OF TRAINING

The complete exercise for deer tracking is split into two phases. The first phase is for your Wirehair to track a blood trail successfully, the second is to communicate success in finding deer to the handler. Communication is normally done by either the 'Bringselverweiser' or the 'Totverbeller' method. In general terms, the Bringselverweiser method involves a dog, who has successfully found the deer, returning to the handler carrying an object (Bringsel) by mouth and leading the handler back to the find. The Totverbeller is where a dog is taught to speak (bark) on finding the deer and to remain there, still speaking, to guide the handler to the find. The latter method is by far the most striking and impressive but it is also more difficult to teach, consequently the first method is the more popular.

BRINGSELVERWEISER

The literal translation of this term is to return with a bringsel (object) on finding where the deer is situated.

It is essential to do all deer tracking work in a collar, so it is advisable to buy a good strong one. Always use the same collar when training, so that your Wirehair soon associates it with working with blood trails and the subsequent finding of deer. You will also need a long lead to attach to the collar and I would suggest that a horse's lunging rope is ideal.

The first task is to obtain a quantity of blood from an abattoir or a friendly local butcher. Ideally, it should be from a freshly killed deer, but at this early stage it can be from any animal. You will need to mix a quantity of salt water to the blood to prevent it coagulating. It has been suggested that the left-overs could be kept frozen in your freezer, but you may wish to visit your source regularly and obtain fresh samples. Another necessity is a deer skin, either freshly killed or one that has been successfully dried. Having acquired these essentials you are now ready to start your first lesson.

It is far easier to begin training in a field, preferably one that you have already used in your basic training. Leave your Wirehair out of sight and, using the blood sample, start to lay a trail. Ensure that you do this so that the wind will be at your dog's back. If your dog works into the wind, there will be a temptation to cut corners on the trail when an airborne scent is picked up. In the early days, it is advisable to leave a small visible marker which will remind you where the trail starts. Use a drop of blood every three feet and ensure that the trail is being laid in a zigzag. This encourages the use of the scent, as happens in quartering, rather than simply following a visual trail that has been laid in a straight line. Do not be too ambitious in the early stages, and make the initial trails quite short. At the end of the trail, place your deer skin on the ground and, if you are using a dried skin, place some blood on the site and on the skin and put a piece of food as a reward on top. When you return to the start, try to remember not to walk directly over the trail you have laid. To help your Wirehair track successfully, it is advisable to leave the blood trail for at least an hour before attempting it, thereby allowing the scent particles to accumulate.

Now go and collect your dog and attach the lunging rope to the collar so that it hangs down the dog's chest. Then feed it between the front legs and out just behind the elbow. You will need to keep hold of the rope at all times, feeding it out and gathering it back as and when required. You should never pull the lead, or use it to indicate direction. Go to the start of the trail and encourage your dog to sniff at the area and take an interest in the new smell. As you are doing this you will need to give a new command, the one you will use throughout the training. Your Wirehair is intelligent enough to realise quite quickly that wearing the same collar and rope and responding to the same command each time, brings the same reward. Hopefully, your Wirehair will start carefully and work steadily, following the trail. If at any time you realise that the trail has been lost, command your dog to sit, then return to the point where the trail was lost and begin again. Never continue in the hope of picking the trail up at a later place; always return to the place where it was lost. Once the skin has been found, let the reward be eaten and do not forget the thorough praise.

Do not overtrain using the blood trails. As with most exercises, dogs in general get bored easily, so confine the blood trail exercise to a maximum of twice a week. As your Wirehair becomes more experienced, you can increase the distance of a trail until it is in excess of several hundred metres. Ring the changes by asking other members of your family to place the trail, and do not always put your Wirehair on a fresh trail – leave it several hours before you start. You can also lay trails in woods, as most of your future work will take place in this terrain. When you start to do this, remember you can use leaves to cover part of the blood trail, as this will encourage your Wirehair to sniff more diligently. You, as the handler, must always know where the trail is and the route it takes.

Never allow any detour from it in order to hunt for other things. When this happens, you must command your dog to sit and then return to the place where the trail was abandoned. This enforces the point that, in order to be a successful deer tracker, only this exercise is allowed, not a combination of this and hunting for other game.

When you feel that your Wirehair is fully competent at finding the deer skin, you can introduce the Bringsel. All exercises from this point on are done without the lunging rope being attached, so it is essential that you are confident of your Wirehair's ability to track successfully. The Bringsel is usually a piece of leather attached to your dog's collar. However, you can use any object, providing it can be properly attached. The point is that, on finding the deer, it must be possible for the Bringsel to be swung into your dog's mouth, so ensure that the object you use is long enough for the dog to be able to do this.

Your initial lesson will be to teach your Wirehair to retrieve your chosen Bringsel. The next stage is to place the Bringsel at the end of a short blood trail; when your Wirehair reaches the end, encourage the retrieve of the Bringsel back to you.

The next stage requires great patience. Lay another blood trail and, at the end, stake out a deer skin but, instead of leaving food as a reward, leave the Bringsel. Cast your Wirehair off at the start of the trail, then follow, as you need to be able to see what happens. Once the skin has been reached, you must encourage the retrieve of the Bringsel. When it is returned to you in your dog's mouth, do not remove it but insist on being led back to the place where the skin is staked out. As soon as you both return to the deer skin, command your dog to go down and, after a short stay, be lavish with the praise.

Weidenhugel Chanute at the successful completion of a blood trail with his owner Aloysia Hard in Germany.

Once you are sure that this exercise has been understood, you can proceed to the next stage which involves attaching the Bringsel to the collar. In the early stage use quite a long piece of cord so that it is in contact with the ground. Repeat the previous exercise, but this time encourage your Wirehair to bring back the Bringsel that is attached to the cord. Only when you can repeatedly complete this exercise can you shorten the cord. The final position of the Bringsel is hanging from the collar, with just sufficient length of cord to allow it to swing into your Wirehair's mouth.

The final part of this exercise is to introduce a freshly shot specimen. This is a test of your training because, if that has been thorough, your Wirehair should continue to perform to standard and return with the Bringsel. However should your dog attack and worry at the specimen, you should stop and return to an earlier exercise.

TOTVERBELLER

The translation of this terms is the dog will bark (bells) on finding the deer, indicating that he has found it.

The ideal dog for this method is one who has a strong character and is not nervous in any way. The object, basically, is to teach your dog to bark on command. One of the easiest methods is to involve food and encourage barking by teasing your dog with it. Repeatedly give the command "speak", withholding the food until you have been obeyed. Obviously, as soon as this happens, give the food as a reward together with lots of praise. You can expand this to include food at meal times. In view of the fact that you are encouraging your dog to bark on command, your next lessons should be conducted in an area where you are not going to inconvenience anybody. What you are trying to achieve is getting your Wirehair to bark for long periods of time without stopping. This is why you need a dog with a strong character, because most will be too sensitive and think they are acting out of line. If you feel that your Wirehair will never be able to speak for long periods of time, then forget this method and concentrate on the Bringselverweiser technique.

The next stage is to introduce a deer skin at the end of a short blood trail, covering a dish

Having tracked down the stag, this Wirehair is communicating to his handler with the Totverbeller method.

of food. Once the deer skin has been found, give the command "Speak"; and as soon as your dog has barked, lift the deer skin and allow the food to be eaten. The next stage is to do this same exercise but without the reward of a dish of food.

Once these exercises have been successfully completed, you then have to persuade your Wirehair to remain at the deer and to speak continuously. Using the lead, go to the place where you have arranged the skin and tie your dog in a way that makes it impossible to lie down. Give the command and then be extremely patient, because you are now encouraging behaviour – that of barking while on a lead – which you have frowned on all through puppyhood as being outrageous. It will take time for your dog to understand this change. Immediately you are obeyed, you must give the reward of freedom from the lead. Extend the time of speaking until your Wirehair is capable of barking for considerable lengths of time.

To help your Wirehair to find the skin, remember to use the command that you gave when starting the blood trails. This command is a reminder that the deer must be found. The next exercise is to set a short blood trail with the skin at the end and cast your Wirehair off, with the usual command. Once the skin has been found, give the command to stay with the skin, and then to speak. As soon as the barking starts, give lots of praise and release your dog. Once this phase has been successfully completed you have instilled the basis of the Totverbeller method.

Increase the distance of the blood trail and vary the locations. Always ensure that you are in a position to follow your dog after the cast-off. This will enable you to be sure of what is happening once the skin has been found and, if you consider that the bark is slow in coming, you will be able to prompt your dog to speak and encourage the stay. In real-life stalks, the time it takes you to reach your Wirehair will vary, so, during training, extend and alter the time of barking to ensure that it is continuous until you release your dog from speaking.

As in the Bringselverweiser method, once you have reached the stage of successful exercises with a skin, you should then introduce an actual deer specimen. Repeat the exercises using the deer instead of a skin, but ensure that you are in a position to see what your Wirehair is doing and be ready to enforce the Speak command if the deer is interfered with.

Whichever method you decide to teach, you will need indescribable patience and unlimited time. This training takes months and, even when you consider that the training is over, you will still need to continue to practise. Only time will tell, when you get into the real thing, how successful the training has been. Take every opportunity of practising on freshly shot deer but be prepared to return to your exercises if you feel that you and your Wirehair are not ready. It is far easier to go back and reinforce a particular exercise than to continue and risk undoing all you have achieved.

FALCONRY

Falconry is the art of hunting game with a trained hawk. A Falconer's main job is to provide the bird with opportunities to hunt and pursue game, which is made far easier with the assistance of a dog.

If you have acquired your Wirehair to accompany you in this ancient art, you will, more

*Chris Soanes and
Bareve Brocade.*

*Chris Soanes and
Ch. Bareve
Bramble at a
successful kill.*

Peter Lomasney with litter sisters Bareve Brocade and Ch. Bareve Bramble taking a breather up on the Scottish moors.

than likely, have purchased your bird first. An important factor in Falconry is to match the right bird to the right person. Factors to be taken into account include the facilities you have, the time you have available for flying and, more important, your temperament. As in most sports which involve training, you need patience and understanding, because complete training of both bird and dog may take a considerable time. This sport is a long-term commitment.

Having found both the Wirehair puppy and the bird of your choice, the main task will be to introduce them to each other. A good rapport between dog and bird must be established. The ideal situation is to let your Wirehair see the bird whilst it is in the safety of the mews (pen). This allows the bird to observe the puppy and the inquisitive puppy to watch the bird from a safe distance and involves no danger to either party. Your Wirehair must learn to respect your bird but must not fear it.

Your Wirehair puppy must have regular association with your bird to allow mutual respect to grow. If you have had your bird for a considerable time, it may have already been introduced to dogs before. If this is not the case, you will have a difficult time ahead, getting both parties to accept each other in close proximity. In view of the fact that you are dealing with a wild bird and a domesticated dog, the Wirehair will probably accept the close presence of the bird before the bird will accept the Wirehair.

Even when your dog is still a puppy, you need to have discipline. You must prevent any attempt to play with the bird. You need to have basic control, plus acceptance of the bird, before you can proceed. In an attempt to get the bird to accept your Wirehair, try feeding it while the puppy is on a stay exercise close by. Also, take your bird on your arm and allow your puppy to roam loose. Initially your bird will spread its wings in an attempt to emphasize its size. Once the bird gets used to your Wirehair moving and satisfies itself that it need not fear the dog, the bird will relax and will normally start to preen itself. When you get to this stage you are well on your way to owning a winning team.

The bird should accompany you as much as possible in the early stages. Do ensure that the bird is kept above your dog's head height, which will increase its feeling of security. Do not allow your Wirehair to walk under your bird when it is on the fist. If you are righthanded and you carry the bird on your left fist, you must teach your Wirehair, right from the onset, to walk on the righthand side. If you continue the introduction between dog and bird when the bird is at its flying weight, it will stimulate the bird's attention and encourage it to watch your Wirehair. This is a good sign for the future when the dog will be actually hunting for game.

Long before you experience the thrill of dog and bird working together, your Wirehair will need to undergo some training. This is actually not too different from the basics that are needed for field trial work. If we look at the basic format, you will be able to concentrate on those specific areas. Your Wirehair will need to hunt and find suitable game, then to point staunchly while your bird is released and climbs to an acceptable height and position. Your Wirehair will then flush the game and remain steady to drop. This enables your bird to dive and, hopefully, catch the game. If, however, your dog chases the game without pointing, or runs in after flushing, the bird's opportunity for a successful catch will be ruined because it will not be in the correct position. False pointing can also be disastrous because, once your bird is in flight and in the correct position, it will expect to be rewarded with food by catching its prey.

As you can see, the two main phases are pointing staunchly and being steady to flush. You can do many exercises to improve steadiness. Start by using dummies. Once your Wirehair remains steady to these, try introducing an item of game instead of one of the dummies.

Pointing is totally hereditary and natural. If all of your previous training has been done on a piece of ground that has been relatively free from game, you will need to introduce some game to encourage your dog to point. Remember, if you doubt initially whether the points will be held, be ready with the lead, give steadying commands, flush the game yourself and insist that your dog sits and does not run in. Wirehairs do vary on pointing. Invariably puppies point many things but, as training increases and new and interesting things are introduced, it can become unreliable. Do not be dismayed, it is all part of growing up. Remember that if your Wirehair used to point as a youngster, that ability will return.

Prior to actually flying your bird free with your Wirehair, you must get both dog and bird familiar with each other during flight. Position your dog reasonably close in a down stay, then call your bird to your fist. This exercise will test your dog's steadiness because, up to this point, all close contact has been while the bird was stationary on your fist. If your Wirehair moves or attempts to chase, then you must delay this exercise. Return to the stay exercises and enforcement of the down whistle. If, however, the flying exercise is successful, carefully decrease the distance of the position of the down stay until your Wirehair is by your side. This will take many days because, in addition to your Wirehair's steadiness, you will have to be guided by the bird's attitude and its speed of acceptance. If your bird becomes agitated, go back to the previous stage until it relaxes. Provided all the early introductions have been successful, they should both readily accept each other in this exercise.

The same principle can be adopted when you are calling the bird to the lure. Initially, ensure that there is quite a distance between your Wirehair (who should be in a down stay) and yourself whilst you are calling the bird to the lure. Once this is successful, decrease the distance until your Wirehair is lying quietly by the bird whilst it is feeding on the lure. This is useful practice because, when you are out hunting, you may not able to see the bird on its quarry. You then have to cast your Wirehair out, to quarter until the bird is located and then lie down by its side. This makes a much larger target for the Falconer to find.

Once you feel that you have taught your Wirehair enough and your bird is at the correct flying weight, you can put all your training into practice. Cast your Wirehair out to quarter into the wind. If you are fortunate to have a large piece of land, you may have to work in strips, taking several runs to cover it fully. As your Wirehair is quartering, your bird should be alert and watching every move.

When your dog finds game and proceeds to point, make sure that the bird is sitting free on your fist. Do not fly the bird off the back of your dog, stand at least two or three yards away, as this gives the bird a more gradual slope to the quarry. It also stops you disturbing the quarry. As soon as you feel everything is ready, give the commands to flush and drop and release the bird. If the flight has been successful, call your Wirehair to your side first before calling your bird to your fist. If your bird is being awkward, then command your dog to stay a distance away and proceed on your own to retrieve your bird.

I find watching a Falconer at work with a Wirehair very exciting. However, words cannot describe the feeling when it is actually your own dog that is helping a Falconer achieve a successful hunt.

WORKING TRIALS
There are a lot of Wirehairs competing in Working Trials in America, but in Great Britain they are few and far between.

Working Trials should not be confused with Field Trials and Working Tests. In Working Trials, the nosework exercises involve human beings and not the scent of game, and the other exercises centre around control and the agility of the dogs.

The primary aim of the competitor in Working Trials is to obtain seventy per cent of the marks in each group of exercises and eighty per cent of the overall marks available in the stake. If this mark is achieved in an Open Working Trial, the dog is awarded a Certificate of Merit. However, if the mark is achieved at a Championship Trial, the dog may append the qualification to its registered name in one of the following forms:-

CD EX:	Companion Dog Excellent
UD EX:	Utility Dog Excellent
WD EX:	Working Dog Excellent
TD EX:	Tracking Dog Excellent
PD EX:	Patrol Dog Excellent

A dog which achieves the desired standard in a particular stake may progress to a higher stake. In addition to the qualification certificates, awards are usually made for first to fourth in each stake. A dog which is placed first on two occasions in the Tracking Dog stake and/or the Patrol Dog stake at a Championship Trial, is awarded the title of Working Trials Champion (WT CH), providing the dog has gained the necessary marks to be given an excellent grading on the same occasions.

The various exercises required will depend on the individual stake entered, but are split into various stages. Control and stay exercises are: two-minute sit stay with handler out of sight, ten-minute down stay with handler out of sight, a recall exercise, heelwork at normal, fast and slow paces, retrieve a dumb-bell, speak on command, steadiness to gunshot, and a sendaway exercise with distances varying from thirty yards to three hundred yards, depending on the stake. In TD and PD stakes re-direction is added to the sendaway exercise.

The exercises within the agility section are not normally started until your Wirehair is eighteen months old, to guard against potential damage to the developing bone structure. The actual exercises require a dog to clear a six-foot scale, stay and wait for recall, a nine-foot long jump and a three-foot clear jump.

The nosework section is split into track and search exercises. In general a Working Trial dog must be trained to pick up any article with human scent on it. The track exercise carries over 50 per cent of the total marks. Each dog has a fresh piece of ground, as the ground may not be used more than once in twenty-four hours. Some time earlier, a tracklayer will have walked around a field, for approximately half a mile, without crossing his tracks, and left articles in accordance with a pattern set by the judge. The dog is expected to follow where the tracklayer has walked. In the UD stake the track is at least thirty minutes old and the dog will be required to find and retrieve one article. In the WD stake the track is one and a half hours old and two articles are expected to be retrieved. The PD stake track is two hours old and two articles are to be found and retrieved, and in the TD stake, the track is three hours old and three articles are required to be found.

The terrain may be grass, heather, plough, winter wheat, set-aside or whatever ground is available. The dog is worked on a harness to which a line is attached and, usually, has between fifteen and twenty minutes to complete the track. The start is normally indicated by a pole. The search area is twenty-five yards square, marked out by poles at each corner. Four articles, all supplied by the judge, are hidden within this area. The dog has five minutes to retrieve the articles without the handler entering the square. The dog must recover at least two out of the four articles to qualify. Marks are lost for dropping or chewing the articles or fouling the square. The patrol section in the Patrol Stake involves manwork exercises including quarter and search for missing persons, chase and attack and test of courage. In Great Britain there are no Wirehairs competing in this stake at present. Expert advice about requirements should be sought before attempting the patrol exercises. These skills should only be taught when the handler has a high degree of control over the dog.

WIREHAIRS IN WORKING TRIALS
Wirehairs are wonderful tracking dogs and natural athletes, which should make them an ideal breed for Working Trials. Unfortunately, they have a very highly developed hunting

Benreeda Wolfgang of Jacinto CD EX, UD EX, WD EX, TD EX: The most successful Wirehair in Working trials in the UK, to date.

instinct and can be very wilful, coupled with being very sensitive on occasions.

The most successful Wirehair in Working Trials in Great Britain to date is Terry Hadley's Benreeda Wolfgang of Jacinto CD EX, UD EX, WD EX, and TD EX. Bred by Mrs Pat Dempster and sired by Bareve Baltimore of Benreeda out of Anka of Roland Rat at Benreeda, Hogan already has one Working Trials CC, which he won at Scarborough in August 1993 from an entry of 105 dogs in the TD stake. Terry Hadley rates Hogan's nosework abilities very highly, and it is considered only a matter of time before this dog gains his full title.

Other Wirehairs have achieved success in Working Trials. Mrs Judith Simpson's black and white dog, Wolfgang of Woodram, bred by Mrs Lynn Briggs and sired by Wittekind Briggs out of Lanka Bertha vom Insul enjoyed a fair amount of success in the 1980s and qualified to work WD stake at Championship Working trials. Deb Berriman's dog Springbok Wood has obtained a COM and a second place in the CD stake at the North East Counties open trial in February 1993. Also Miss Anne Cook's bitch Unique Ulla has regularly competed in Working trials, gaining a COM and first prize in the CD stake at the North West Working Trials Open trial in December 1992. In September 1993, Hazel, as she is known, achieved a COM and first prize in the UD stake at the Yorkshire Working Trials open trial. She has now added the titles CD EX and UD EX to the list of her accomplishments. Anne claims that Hazel has not been the easiest dog to train and has lots of ability, especially when it comes to tracking. Unfortunately she has a naughty habit of switching off and quartering the field for any game, when she should be doing a sendaway in a nice straight line and stopping and

Cadenberg Filou v Lutz CDX, TD competing in the US.

recalling when she is told! However, she is now showing signs of maturing but Anne finds her too clever by half and is constantly seeking ways of convincing her that the exercises should be done Anne's way.

The Wirehairs in America were competing in our equivalent of Working trials in the mid 1950s. The first details of a Wirehair being successful in this sphere was in 1956 when Hilde. Hilverheide, owned by Mr and Mrs J.C. Moore, Jnr, qualified for a CD award. This was followed by another CD award gained by Oldenmills Mica, owned by J.H. Schuecking.

In the mid 1960s Am. Can. Ch. Haar Baron's Lise Von Graeta, owned by Betty Graettinger, gained the first CDX award together with a UD degree. During 1967 Dual Ch. Haar Baron's Tina, owned by D.H. Faestel became the first Dual to win a CD award. Wolf Floege-Boehm's Dual Ch. Queen Vom Stoppelsberg. a German import, became the first Wirehair Dual to win the CDX award. Joanne Kutsch's Arras Zur Wolfschlucht, who was bred by Wolf Floege-Boehm out of a litter from Diane Zur Wolfschlucht, a daughter of Dual Ch. Queen Vom Stoppelsberg, and Suzette Wood's Am. Ch. Hilltop's Shula of Bogay, both

Am. Ch. Meadow Valley's Blitz-Krieg CD, owned by Bobby Applegate.

attained the TD award during the 1970s. The most successful two exhibitors in Working Trials in America have been Suzette Wood and Ray Hennum. They are the only exhibitors to date who have achieved UD awards with more than one Wirehair. The best-known Wirehair of recent time has been Ray Hennum's Am. Can Ch. Obedience Trial Ch. Nordic's Viking Brandy, Can. CDX.

AGILITY TESTS

The English Kennel Club considers agility tests to be fun competitons designed for enjoyment by the competitors, their dogs and the spectators. Agility was first introduced as a demonstration at Cruft's dog show in 1978. It is now so popular in the UK that it is not unusual for there to be over five hundred entries in one class, if that class happens to be a qualifier for a major event such as Olympia. There are two types of tests: agility classes and jumping classes. In agility classes, all the Kennel Club recognised obstacles may be used. However, in the jumping classes, the contact point equipment – that is, "A" frame, dog walk and see-saw – are excluded.Penalities are incurred for knocking down fences, for refusals and for failing to make contact at the proper points. There is also a standard course time, with time faults added to jumping faults.

The training falls into three broad categories:-

1. SPEED AND CONTROL The faster the dog can negotiate the two-foot-six inch hurdles and the ground between the obstacles, the better the chance of winning. This calls for split second timing and absolute obedience to get the dog to turn in the right direction on command.

2. CONFIDENCE Initially the dog may be apprehensive of obstacles such as the "A" frame, dog walk and tunnels. Once the dog is confident about these obstacles, the problem will be to prevent them being done at the wrong time.

3. SKILL OBSTACLES The skill obstacles include the see-saw, tyre and weaving poles and require considerable practice. Few see-saws will tip at exactly the same place and few tyres are identical. The dog will need experience to be able to cope with the wide range of see-saws and tyres at the shows. The most practice will be needed teaching the weaving poles. A good dog will eventually enter the poles from any direction, ahead of the handler, and weave independently.

It is considered that a reasonable level of control should be achieved before teaching a dog agility. Additionally, all dogs should be well over twelve months of age before the teaching starts and should not be jumped extensively under eighteen months of age.

There are only a few Wirehairs in the UK that have competed in agility. Most recently Trish Yates' bitch Othamcourt Hattie, sired by Stablaheim Dorne out of Wittekind Heidi Gazis, has put in some good rounds. Also, Unique Ulla is competing regularly and is managing to achieve some clear rounds within the course time. To date she has won a sixth place in a Novice jumping competition despite, during her early competitions, preferring to leave the ring in search of rabbits!

DRUG DETECTION DOGS

This is a very specialised field and it is only now, in the UK, that the Police force, the Army

Am. Ch. Heywire's Windstorm at six and a half months, before he joined the Maryland State Police.

and the Royal Air Force are realising that the Wirehair could be very useful. The breed's scenting ability and desire to work, coupled with extreme intelligence, has proved to be successful in the detection of drugs and explosives. A few Wirehairs have been taken into various training establishments in several countries and, having successfully completed the detailed training, have been accepted. The most outstanding Wirehair to date in this sphere has been Am. Ch. Heywire's Wind Storm, bred by Judy Cheshire and Beverly Murray.

THERAPY DOGS

Both in the United Kingdom and the United States of America there are Wirehairs who are certified therapy dogs. They possess exceptional temperaments and will allow people who are in hospital, or in homes, to fuss them and generally love them.

One of the most successful therapy dogs is Am. Ch. Medow Valley's Blitz-Krieg CD. Blitz is a truly versatile dog who has achieved his Show Championship, his CD award and NAVHDA working qualifications, and is a certified therapy dog.

Blitz successfully qualified at nine and a half months in the NAVHDA natural ability test. He finished his Show Championship at twenty-three months of age with all majors, together with his CD award. At three years of age Blitz qualified in the NAVHDA Utility test. In between times he visits nursing homes regularly and his speciality is to carry a basket filled with cookies to distribute among the residents. This special feat has earned him several television appearances.

Chapter Fourteen

COMMON AILMENTS

Good health does not happen naturally but needs to be nurtured from puppyhood and maintained with care throughout your dog's life. Sensible diet, regular exercise and husbandry, coupled with regular vaccinations, wormings and the necessary veterinary check-ups, are the basic essentials of good health and are the responsibility of the owner.

As far as good health is concerned, dogs are no different to humans. At any time of their life they may experience illness through either hereditary weakness or by an accident or through a virus. Most dogs will also suffer the odd bout of vomiting, sometimes combined with diarrhoea, and have days where they seem not to be at their best. If you feel that your Wirehair is 'off colour', for whatever reason, then it is essential that you seek veterinary advice. It is sensible to be on the cautious side rather than leave your Wirehair until a more serious problem or illness emerges. Do not try to treat everything yourself as, in most cases, a visit to your veterinary surgeon will be all that's needed. I have listed below some common problems that seem to occur in German Wirehaired Pointers. Some are hereditary and some are not. However, with reference to those which are hereditary, it is essential for both breeders and owners to be truthful. In most cases breeders do try to produce Wirehairs that are free from any hereditary problems. Unfortunately because the breed is a relatively new one, with several different strains of foundation stock, breeders will not always know what might happen with a litter.

Therefore both breeders and owners have an obligation to the German Wirehaired Pointer breed to 'come clean' and admit to any hereditary problems which may have occurred and to do their utmost to prevent them being repeated in subsequent litters. This is the only way to safeguard the breed's future and to prevent owners having the upset of losing their Wirehair tragically young. Consequently, if you have the breed's future at heart, do not bury your head in the sand at the mention of any hereditary problem, just be truthful and join the fight to keep the Wirehair as problem-free as possible.

ALOPECIA: This is a skin condition which results in a complete loss of hair right down to the follicles. The odd patches of alopecia that appear in older dogs are not normally cause for concern. However, extensive areas of complete hair loss in dogs that are considerably younger will need veterinary attention, because this is often associated with hormonal disturbances or an incorrect diet.

BLOAT: Bloat is commonly known as gastric torsion or gastric dilation. The reason for this life-threatening condition is still virtually unknown. It usually seems to affect the larger, deep-chested breeds but there have been cases of the Wirehair being affected. Stress, over-feeding, exercising immediately after feeding, and fermentation of ingested food are all possible causes of bloat. The initial indications are restlessness quickly followed by frequent attempts to vomit that either produce nothing at all or, in some cases, a white frothy liquid. The dog becomes very uncomfortable and in some cases you will actually be aware of your dog becoming bloated and pot-bellied. If you think there is a possibility of bloat, you must not delay but must go to your veterinary surgeon immediately, because it is a life or death situation. The most serious part of bloat is when the stomach twists up to 180 degrees. This is torsion, which, at the very least, causes an incredible amount of pain – but in many cases death is inevitable because no gas or fluid can escape once the stomach twists. Even with rapid veterinary attention the survival rate is extremely low.

To try and prevent bloat from occurring it is advisable to feed your dog's daily food allowance in two separate meals. Feeding should never take place immediately after strenuous exercise and no exercise should be allowed for at least two hours after each feed.

EAR PROBLEMS: The Wirehair suffers considerably with excessive hair growth in the ear canal. Those Wirehairs with the appealing hairy faces and masses of whiskers will have the same hairy inner ears. It is therefore essential that, right from an early age, you insist that your puppy allows ear inspections. As soon as the hair becomes long enough for you to be able to grasp it with your fingers, you must start to remove it. If you cannot get a grip on the waxy hair, take a piece of tissue and wrap that around the tip of the hair, which should enable you to pull it out. Make sure that you only remove a small amount at first, so that you do not make your Wirehair fear the procedure. If you do not start early enough your Wirehair will resent you attempting to remove the hair and you will have to resort to visits to your veterinary surgeon who will probably have to use a general aneasthetic.

If you leave the hair in the ear canal it will become overheated, which may cause an infection. If that is left untreated, ulceration will occur. Ear infections will also cause your Wirehair to scratch excessively and that, coupled with head shaking, may produce a haematoma which will require veterinary treatment.

ECTROPION AND ENTROPION: Ectropion is a condition in which one or both eyelids are turned outward so that the conjunctiva is exposed. The eyes continually water and this usually forms a mark down the side of the dog's cheeks.

Entropion is where the eyelids turn inwards and the eyelashes make contact with the eyeball. This causes inflammation and irritation which make the dog continually blink. Entropion is the more common of the two conditions.

In both cases surgical correction is necessary to allow the dog to lead a normal life-style. These conditions are not life-threatening, just a nuisance. However, most veterinary surgeons will not operate until the dog is at least six months old. If only one operation is required to alleviate the problem then, as soon as the stiches are removed, your dog should not experience any more problems.

The conditions are considered to be hereditary, so any Wirehairs who have received corrective surgery for either ectropion or entropion should never be bred from, and the KC registration should be endorsed accordingly. Unfortunately some unscrupulous breeders and owners have their stock operated on and, once the signs have disappeared, will either sell them on to owners without informing them of the operation, or will breed with the dogs themselves and run the risk of producing more stock with these eye complaints.

FITS: Fits can be caused by a number of things ranging from epilepsy to hysteria, and can vary enormously with regard to visible signs and duration.

Establishing the cause of any fit or convulsion is a job for your vet. It is a complex subject which needs thorough investigation before any diagnosis can be reached. You can help by collecting as much information about your dog's life-style before, during and after any occurrence that could be classed as a fit. It is very frightening to watch a dog having convulsions and the only consolation is that the dog will probably be unconscious during the seizure and not really aware what is happening.

As I have just said, it is a complex subject and you must not jump to conclusions as to the cause. Epilepsy is probably everybody's first thought, but an attack of hysteria could be the possible reason for an isolated fit. Whatever the cause, you must be guided by your own vet, who will endeavour to establish the real root of the problem. The prescription of drugs will be necessary in an attempt to keep the fits under control and allow both the dog and the owner to lead a relatively normal life. In view of the seriousness of the problem it is advisable never to breed from a dog who has suffered from a series of fits or from any of the dog's close relatives.

HIP DYSPLASIA: This is a condition in which either the femur or the hip socket or both are abnormal and are prevented from fitting together properly, resulting in varying types of dysplasia. For example the socket may be too shallow for the head of the femur or the femur head may be mis-shapen.

To evaluate the degree of hip dysplasia, dogs are put under general anaesthetic and have their hips X-rayed. The X-rays are then assessed and scored by a panel of expert radiographic veterinary surgeons. In the UK X-rays can be taken from twelve months of age; in the United States a permanent grading is made after the dog is two years of age. Unfortunately, it is no longer possible for veterinary surgeons to take hip X-rays without general anaesthetic. It is considered preferable to sedate the dog in this way, rather than expose the owner, who would normally want to hold the dog during examination, to excessive radiation. This now means that fewer people are submitting their dogs for hip X-rays, because quite a high proportion of dogs cannot tolerate general anaesthetic, and fail to regain consciousness. Owners realise that, with life-threatening conditions, general anaesthetics are necessary and the chance is worth taking; however, many feel that to subject their dogs to this risk, just to have hips X-rayed, is not justified.

There are many differing theories about the cause of hip dysplasia, from it being totally hereditary to it being caused by overfeeding, wrong diet or too much exercising. Whatever the reason, it is essential to keep in mind the necessity for overall soundness in what is a working gundog breed. However, we must keep a sense of proportion and realise that hips alone are not the most important feature of the Wirehair.

HYPOTHYROIDISM: The thyroid is a ductless gland situated in the dog's neck which secretes thyroxine, an essential product providing some of the nutrition needed for all parts of the dog's body and in particular the hair. A lack of thyroxine usually makes dogs become lethargic and easily tired which, in turn, can cause obesity in the older dog. The skin becomes dry, and extensive symmetrical hair loss coupled with thickening, darker skin may occur. Hypothyroidism can be treated with a daily oral treatment, which will be needed for the rest of the dog's life.

PHANTOM PREGNANCY: Phantom pregnancy does seem to be a fairly common problem with the Wirehair. There is no set pattern, as it can occur at the first season or just develop at a later season and can either be a mild or a full-blown phantom. A full-blown phantom pregnancy is quite obvious, as the bitch will exhibit all the classic signs of labour, making a bed, carrying toys around and nestling with them, whistling and shivering, and almost certainly she will go off all food. Her undercarriage will develop and fill up with milk, and in severe cases the milk will drip and ooze from the teats.

In mild cases the bitch will probably make a bed and carry around some of her toys; she will more than likely refuse her food, but although her undercarriage will develop, it is unlikely that she will actually leak milk from her teats. With the mild cases the simplest solution is to ignore the bitch and her symptoms and just keep offering her food until she decides that she has passed the worse stage. However, with the more serious cases you will need to consult your veterinary surgeon for his advice. Unfortunately most phantom pregnancies will generally affect the coat and resulting hair loss is not unusual.

Prevention is difficult: I have found that once a bitch has a phantom pregnancy she will continue to have them at every season. Vets sometimes suggest that bitches should have a litter and this will stop the problem. However, I do not agree with this view, because those of our own bitches who are susceptible to phantom pregnancies have continued to have them even after producing litters. The only infallible cure is to have your bitch spayed. If you are not considering having a litter from your bitch, then this is the most sensible solution. However, if you wish to retain the option of a possible future litter, then you will just have to manage until after the event and then consider having your bitch spayed.

PYOMETRA: Pyometra is a collection of pus in the womb and it often develops shortly after a season. There are two types of pyometra, closed or open, the difference being that a discharge is seen in an open pyometra. The first signs are that your bitch will seem to be off colour and will start to drink excessively. There may be a vaginal discharge but in the closed type the bitch's abdomen will become distended instead. If these signs are overlooked and neglected your bitch will become toxic and will start to vomit.

The only treatment is to have an emergency spaying which should include the removal of the ovaries. Providing you act upon the early signs, the success rate is high. However, when the bitch enters the toxic stage, the success rate becomes considerably lower.